A Long Way, Baby

Grace Lichtenstein

A Long Way, Baby

BEHIND THE SCENES IN WOMEN'S PRO TENNIS

Photography by Nancy Moran

WILLIAM MORROW & COMPANY, INC.
NEW YORK   1974

Printed in the United States of America.

2 3 4 5   78 77 76 75 74

Book design by Helen Roberts

Library of Congress Cataloging in Publication Data

Lichtenstein, Grace.
  A long way, baby.

  1. Tennis.   2. Tennis—Biography.   I. Title.
GV999.L52   796.34′2   74-1166
ISBN 0-688-00263-3

For my mother,
Rose Rosenthal,
who couldn't play the game
but always knew the score

Acknowledgments

To begin with, I'm indebted to all the friends and associates who contributed scores of suggestions in the Great Title Sweepstakes. Among my favorite rejects are *Tennis Without Balls; Nylons or Gut; Lob in the Afternoon; Curve and Volley; Deep Stroke; Under the Net; Ladies of the Court; Game, Set, Snatch; High-Heeled Sneakers; They Also Serve* and *Women in Love.* The sweepstakes winner was Dan Johnson. Special mention to Steve Lichtenstein, the witty pornographer.

The sportswriters on the tennis circuit were more than generous with their time and gave me invaluable insight into the game. My thanks to, among others, Bud Collins of the *Boston Globe,* Dave Gray of the *Guardian,* Laurie Pignon of the *Daily Mail,* David Hirshey of the New York *News,* Ron Bookman of *World Tennis* and, most of all, Neil Amdur of *The New York Times.*

Several of my editors at the *Times* helped pay my way by assigning me to tennis stories during the year: Arthur Gelb, Mike Levitas, Jim Tuite, Frank Litsky and Harvey Shapiro. I'm also grateful to John Rockwell, Walter Lippincott and Caroline Seebohm for the Astrodome tapes; to Laurie and Steve Dankner for their musical vocabulary; and to Dr. Kiev, Dr Pepper, Jack Daniels, John Wayne, John Ford, The Thousand Eyes, Wilson Pickett, Creedence Clearwater Revival, Diana Ross, the Rolling Stones and

Acknowledgments

Three Dog Night, who helped sustain me through the long season.

No list of thank-yous would be complete without mentioning Jim Landis, who made the connection between tennis and me; Wendy Weil, my agent; Nancy Moran, my photographer; and Jean Kidd, my indefatigable typist. I owe a particular debt of gratitude to Joni Evans of Morrow, the only editor I know who bakes gingerbread for her writers.

Finally, this book would not have been possible without the cooperation of the players themselves, their families and their associates in the tennis world. To each of them, my sincerest thanks.

Contents

Photographs appear between pages 66 and 67 and pages 178 and 179.

Introduction

A FOURTEEN-YEAR-OLD GIRL DASHED UP TO ME OUTSIDE the gates of the West Side Tennis Club, clutching a Billie Jean King model racquet. "I saw you talkin' to the players," she said breathlessly. "You know them? You know Rosie Casals and Billie Jean King?"

Sure, I said. I was writing a book about them.

"Oh, man, they're terrific," she exclaimed. She was a skinny street urchin from Astoria, Queens, who sneaked into the club every day to see the United States Open, badgering the women pros to give her lessons.

"Some day I'm gonna be in there," she said with a defiant wave at the stadium. "Some day I'm gonna be a champ like Billie Jean King!"

I knew exactly how she felt. If I were fourteen years old again, I'd want to be a tennis champ, too. That was one reason I set out to do this book. For the past several years, I'd turned green with envy every time I saw Billie Jean and the rest of the women pros play. I was curious to see, up close, whether the life of a touring professional was really glamorous, whether spending each day in the sun smashing tennis balls for thousands of dollars in exotic cities was the ideal existence it seemed.

There was another reason, too. I viewed Billie Jean King and her colleagues as true pioneers of the women's movement. They were a new breed of career women, who were carving out a place for themselves in what, throughout history, had been strictly a man's world—that of the sports superstar.

Yes, there had been great women athletes in the past: Babe Didrikson Zaharias in golf, Helen Wills Moody, Maureen Connolly, Althea Gibson in tennis. But there had never been a whole *class* of stars as there were now. Moreover, with few exceptions, the greats of the past in tennis and other sports had insisted on being regarded as amateurs. They were expected to retire gracefully from the sporting scene—preferably at the peak of their careers—to settle down with husbands and spawn babies. Those who did become pros, like Zaharias, were generally considered freaks.

As a kid growing up in the 1950's, I accepted the concept of women athletes as freaks. Raised in Brooklyn three blocks from Ebbets Field, I was a passionate Dodger fan, and my earliest career ambition was to replace Carl Furillo in right field. By the time I was twelve, though, I had given up the idea, partly because I couldn't hit a curve but mainly because I had been taught that to want to become an athlete of any kind was unacceptable. Girls were passive, noncompetitive, dependent. Also, there were no women athletes with whom I could identify. I saw Zaharias in a movie once. She struck me as large and mannish. To me, then, the notion of a sexy woman athlete was a contradiction.

I never gave up my love of sports, although as an adult it was from a spectator's point of view, not a participant's. When I became a reporter for *The New York Times* I occasionally got the chance to interview male athletes and I got a charge out of impressing them with my baseball or football expertise. But my first reaction to them was always, "My, how *big* you are." Staring up at the broad shoulders of Jim Bouton, Johnny Unitas or Ron Swoboda, I felt just as tiny as I had when I had taken Duke Snider's picture on Camera Day at Ebbets Field years before. These guys weren't just athletes, they weren't just men. They were a different *species*.

Then, one evening, I wangled an assignment to cover

a tennis exhibition for the benefit of the Women's Political Caucus. I needed a quote from Billie Jean King. Just before her match, I caught her waiting behind the court. I walked over with my notebook to ask a few questions.

The revelation was at hand. For God's sake, I thought to myself, standing beside her, she's no bigger than I am! Here she is, the most charismatic superstar in women's sports, and she's just another short girl with glasses!

Well, I am a short girl, and I wear glasses, and it suddenly dawned on me that Billie Jean King epitomized the revolution women's tennis had built out of the old conflict between athletics and femininity.

I had avidly followed the growth of women's professional tennis since its beginnings in 1968, but I had never thought about its real impact. I began to realize that it was, and is, a feminist breakthrough.

The women pros were as nice to look at as they were to watch perform, generally graceful, well-proportioned girls who showed the sports public they could be tough without being mannish. Women like Billie Jean King and Nancy Richey Gunter made tomboyishness acceptable . . . even sexy. A few players—Wendy Overton, Kristien Kemmer, Julie Anthony—were quite beautiful. And one, Christine Marie Evert, was so cute, youthful and poised she had replaced the movie ingenue as the traditional American dream girl.

More importantly, these women were defying all the false tenets of femininity that had plagued me and so many other girls. It was their *job* to compete, to push themselves to the limit of their aggressiveness. Thomas Boslooper, in his book *The Femininity Game,* noted that most women were brought up to be losers. "They're brainwashed," he wrote. "They don't know how to win because they've been conned and coerced from infancy into believing they shouldn't try. . . . Women have succeeded in liberating their intellects, but their bodies are still in corsets."

Yet, for Billie Jean King and the rest of the tennis pros, the only goal in life was to win.

This book is the record of the 1973 women's tennis circuit, as seen through selected tournaments, minor as well as major.*

During the year, I traveled with the players in the United States and England, ate with them, drank with them, rooted for them and suffered with them. And I learned from them.

The first thing I learned was a very personal lesson that should serve as a warning to other weekend hackers. My father (a chip-and-dink shot artist in the Bitsy Grant-Bobby Riggs tradition) had taught me to play tennis when I was a child. At the start of the year, I nurtured the delusion that maybe, just maybe, if I had been born ten years later, if I had played more tennis and less stickball, I might have gotten good enough to be a pro. The women's game looked *easy,* damn it! (Of course, that's the attraction of both tennis and golf—they are both games in which spectators con themselves into thinking they can play the pros. A middle-aged man can't picture himself in Larry Csonka's Number 39 jersey when he watches the Dolphins on the football field, because the brute physical gap is too wide. But that same man watching Arnold Palmer? Ah, he feels the putter in his grip, his knees bend to measure the slope of the green . . . and for a moment, he sincerely believes he's in Arnie's shoes.)

At the start of the year, I sincerely believed that with rigorous training, I could be in Billie Jean's shoes.

---

* Although it ends, for obvious reasons, in Houston in September, there were several major developments during the fall: Chris Evert won her second Virginia Slims championship in a row at the pro circuit finale in Boca Raton in Florida in October, then later won the Commercial Union grand prix (a prize based on a system of assigning points to victories at various tournaments throughout the year) by sweeping the South African championship in November. Margaret Court was ranked Number 1 woman player in the world in November for her 1973 performances. Rosemary Casals, throughout her career a consistent loser to Billie Jean King, scored two impressive wins over King within two months. And an Australian team led by Evonne Goolagong beat the Americans, led by Chris Evert, in the Bonne Bell Cup in Sydney in December.

(Actually, I was. I went out and bought a pair of BJK-model Adidas.) The pros didn't seem to be terribly swift on their feet, their strokes didn't seem overpowering. Hell, I said to myself one day in St. Petersburg, anybody can play this game. Right?

Wrong.

It was not Billie Jean King, nor Rosie Casals nor Margaret Court, who humbled me, but Nancy Spencer, one of the lowliest of the low qualifiers, the kind of player who never makes the main draw. She led me out onto a green clay court that day in St. Pete, and like a nice teaching pro, started sending balls straight to me. Relentlessly, her clean, flat strokes streaked over the net. Gamely, I sent them blooping back. Why wasn't my fine topspin forehand working? Why were the balls to my backhand bouncing off the wood instead of the gut? Why were my feet so hot I felt as if I were standing on a pancake griddle? *What was I doing here anyway?*

When I quit, huffing and puffing, after twenty minutes, I consoled myself by reasoning that Nancy Spencer probably couldn't write a news story any better than I could play pro tennis.

If I learned some hard lessons from the players, I also learned valuable ones from other reporters. Before the year began I had never been a sportswriter, simply a news writer. Nor, for that matter, had I ever watched tennis the way a sportswriter does. In the beginning, I felt totally inadequate as I watched my *Times* colleague, Neil Amdur, jot down all kinds of incomprehensible numbers during a match and then translate them into a smooth critique of the event for the next day's paper. During post-match interviews with players I listened, dumbstruck, as reporters fired off questions about "that crosscourt backhand in the fourteenth game . . . eight straight points before she wrong-footed you . . . down 4-2 in the third . . . the slice was giving you trouble. . . ."

Where had I been all the time those fascinating things were happening? I had watched a tennis match between two young women, noted the athletic grace of their strokes and the emotions that registered on their faces, had studied what kind of soda they reached for in the cooler between games, and written down the score at the end.

These men, on the other hand (and they were all men, always, except when Billie Jean played Bobby Riggs and women reporters surfaced), had apparently seen a sporting event that rivaled a Beethoven symphony in depth, subtlety and complexity.

Eventually, I became convinced that for my purposes it was just as well I lacked their analytic skill. The people who asked me about women's tennis never asked about that crosscourt backhand at 40-love in the third set of some long-forgotten match. They asked if Chris Evert had a boyfriend and how Billie Jean felt about women's lib.

I think I can now see some of those subtleties the sportswriters see in a match. But I'm no longer envious of their superior knowledge. I was able to approach the women and their game from a different perspective and, hopefully, with a fresher eye.

I asked Chris about her boyfriend (she was engaged to him by the year's end) and I asked Billie Jean about women's lib. I also asked a lot of questions about brassieres and menstrual periods and marijuana and Lesbians and women-as-losers. This book is about those things as well as about playing tennis. At first, I was keenly disappointed that the players' feminist consciousness was not higher than it was. Most of them didn't seem to grasp what it meant to have a pack of adoring little girls (as well as boys, and adults) following them around. Before long, however, I realized the astonishing point about these players was that they were jocks first, women second. For months it disturbed me that they referred to themselves as "girls," until I understood they were using the word the same way men used "guys."

I soon discovered that this was a unique congregation of women—a cross between a sorority and a summer camp, a team and a tribe, a jock sisterhood. I was moved by the genuine respect and affection they had for one another. (As a general rule, according to tennis insiders, the women got along much better than their male equivalents.) They handled themselves the way men on teams do—forming close friendships, bitching about one another, keeping up a perpetual banter in the locker room, sometimes spending more time than they might have preferred in each other's company because of the exigency of being on the road. All this, despite the fact that day after day, night after night, they were pitted against one another on opposite sides of the net.

So many of the players were very young—under twenty-five—that they knew no other adult life but that of tennis touring. They were globe-trotters who saw too many airports and too few museums, grown-ups who were too often treated like children, wage-earners with only rare chances to spend their paychecks. In other words, just jocks.

I got to like them a great deal. It didn't matter to me that they were not glib interview subjects, because their lives spoke eloquently for them. They didn't know much about feminism on an intellectual level, but in their gut they had the rest of us beat two sets to love. Even though they lived in a narrow, insulated, incestuous and sometimes petty little world, they had, as a group, a fine sense of themselves as sports entertainers. They put on few airs; indeed, the visit at one tournament of someone they considered a *real* celebrity, O. J. Simpson, threw a bunch of young players into a giggly dither. They worked terribly hard at their craft, putting themselves on the line day after day in a game that requires self-imposed discipline and does not permit excuses.

Perhaps most importantly, each day they helped knock a few more bricks out of the woman-as-athlete stereotype, helped convince a few more adoring little girls that it was just as okay to want to be Billie Jean King, Superstar, as it was to be Sue Barton, Student Nurse.

Astrotennis

THE HUGE MARQUEE STOOD ON STILTS LIKE AN OVERSIZED pop art sculpture in the middle of a vast empty parking lot on the south edge of Houston. It read: "Wednesday: Baseball Doubleheader—Astros vs. San Diego," and then, in letters almost as high, "Thursday: $100,000 Winner Take All Billie Jean King vs. Bobby Riggs."

In the distance, the landscape was dominated by a massive whitish building with a curved roof—the Astrodome, America's cathedral of sport. Next to it was an oblong green-and-white striped rubber enclosure the size of a Quonset hut, a practice tennis bubble that resembled a caterpillar as conceived by Claes Oldenburg.

The Battle-of-the-Sexes-Match-of-the-Century was about to begin.

Just about everybody who was anybody—Jimmy "The Greek" Snyder, Rod Laver, Bob Hope, the entire sports staff of *The New York Times* and a flock of male and female reporters from all over the globe—knew how it was going to end.

Robert Larimore Riggs, the fifty-five-year-old Peter Pan of tennis, would demolish Billie Jean King in this Texas never-never land, just as he had humiliated her chief rival on the women's pro tennis circuit, Margaret Court, in a far more obscure California never-never land four months before.

21

The odds were 8 to 5 Riggs. I knew, because I had helped make a $500 side bet on behalf of women writers with Bobby himself a few weeks earlier. Nora Ephron, the magazine columnist, and I had haggled Bobby down from even-money at a press conference. At the time, I had a hard time making up my mind whether I'd use my winnings to buy a new tennis racquet or a fall jacket. Now, I had grave doubts about ever seeing the $500 again.

For the past four weeks, Billie Jean had been behaving like a paranoid bitch. She had shut herself off almost completely from the press, refusing nearly all requests for private interviews on the grounds that what counted was what she did on the court, not what she said off it. While Bobby Riggs had basked in the glow of instant celebrityhood, preening at Hollywood restaurants with a starlet on each arm, posing for publicity photos in a Tarzan costume and spouting sexist clichés ("A woman's place is in the bedroom and the kitchen, in that order") that would make Bob Guccione blush, King had dropped out of three major tennis tournaments she had promised to play, injured her fragile right knee, contracted a virus, suffered a fainting spell in the middle of an important match at the U. S. Open, taken blood tests for hypoglycemia and hidden out for the remaining days before the Astrodome affair at her Hilton Head Island villa. A reporter who had seen her in her living room there had described her as the after-picture in a before-and-after advertisement for Seconal.

If ever a woman had looked like a loser the third week in September, 1973, it was Billie Jean King.

At first, she had brushed aside the idea of an intersex match with Riggs, an ebullient has-been who had been making a large part of his living hustling games with amateurs and toiling for penny-ante prizes in sideshow professional senior tennis tournaments, when he had proposed it the previous year. Women's tennis was well on its way to reaching major league sports status, its stars in tax brackets once reserved for the likes of Wilt Chamberlain and Joe

Namath. In 1971, Billie Jean had become the first woman athlete to make more than $100,000 in prize money and then had repeated the feat the following year. At twenty-nine, her wire-rimmed glasses and toothy grin a familiar sight to a burgeoning tennis-loving public, the "Old Lady," as she called herself, was a King by rights as well as by name. "Senior tennis may need us, but women's tennis doesn't need Bobby Riggs," she had said scornfully.

Margaret Court's mind did not work along the same businesslike lines as Billie Jean's. When Bobby Riggs had approached her, she had thought of their match as a cute exhibition for some small change, a nice break in a year of grinding tournament play. Instead, her fourteen-month-old son, Danny, had thrown her sneakers down the toilet and Bobby Riggs had junk-balled his way to fame against her on the same day, in an embarrassing mismatch before a nationwide television audience that was later to be christened the Mother's Day Massacre.

That was in May. In July, a bubbly Billie Jean announced, "Margaret opened the door. Now I'm gonna shut it," and put her signature on a contract that guaranteed the winner of the King-Riggs battle $100,000 plus double that in ancillary rights. She was rather pleased, deep down. It would be the richest, most ballyhooed, most mass-mediaed tennis match in history, and she would be its heroine.

Of course, it had nothing to do with *real* tennis, with the pro sport the women tennis jocks had been building for three years. But that didn't matter. It was the right match in the right place, at the right time, a circus to rank with the Ringling Brothers, a Cecil B. De Mille epic complete with marching bands and dancing bears, a heavyweight fight starring the most quotable athletes since Muhammad Ali. It wasn't tennis, it was Astrotennis, a space-age Hollywood version of the Christians versus the Lions.

Astrotennis even had something the old Colosseum contests hadn't: sex. In purely athletic terms, the match was theater of the absurd, since, as both Billie and Bobby were the first to point out, male tennis pros in their prime could

beat female tennis pros in their prime a hundred times out
of a hundred. Physiology dictated the outcome. The men
were bigger and stronger than the women, just as heavy-
weights were bigger and stronger than featherweights. In
this case, however, physiology had been turned topsy-turvy.
The woman was in her prime, the man was not. The woman
played what was always considered a "man's" style of tennis
—serve and volley; the man played a woman's style—
strategy, dinks, chips and lobs. What had captured the public's imagination had been the challenge implied in Bobby
Riggs's blabbermouthing, that this grand, ludicrous face-off
could somehow settle all the questions posed by women's
liberation.

Margaret Court was more responsible for blowing the
thing out of proportion than Riggs. She had choked against
him, had succumbed to his bag of tricks. The public, un-
aware of her history of falling apart under pressure, reacted
with chauvinistic immediacy: just like a woman. She was
such a nice lady, why didn't she stay home and take care
of her child? the anti-liberationists said. See, darling, what
happens to women who think they can equal men? Be a
good girl and make dinner.

Billie Jean had picked up the fallen standard with ego-
tistical relish. "Bobby's just fighting for money," she declared, "I'm fighting for a cause."

An intersex firecracker had been ignited and it sput-
tered throughout the summer at cocktail parties and at
beach barbecues, in newspaper columns and on the Johnny
Carson show. Sportswriters calmly discussed the merits of
Riggs's lobs versus King's volleys. Husbands made wagers
with wives over who would do the dishes for a week if
Bobby or Billie got beaten. A banker and a trucking company executive in Sulphur, Louisiana, ordered a half-dozen
custom-made "I am a male chauvinist pig" T-shirts and
drove two hundred miles to Houston to sit in the Astrodome
displaying them. Representative Bella Abzug made book
against Riggs with a half-dozen congressmen on the floor
of the House of Representatives.

By midsummer Bobby Riggs was threatening to come

24

on court in a skirt. Billie Jean suggested a mink-lined jock-strap. When I arrived at Houston airport, the young woman at the Avis counter took one look at my tennis racquet, hissed, "I hope she beats the pants off him," and gave me a ten-minute monologue on Sissy Farenthold, Barbara Jordan, and the feminist consciousness of Texas. Things had gotten totally out of hand.

A half-hour's drive from the Astrodome on the outskirts of Houston, workmen were still putting the final coat of shellac on the bleachers at the Net-Set Racquet Club when an unsmiling Billie Jean King walked out onto the center court Monday for her first public tournament match in three weeks.

Long before the Astrodome event had been announced, Virginia Slims, the cigarette company that sponsored one of the two rival women's pro tennis circuits, had scheduled a regular tournament for Houston. Billie Jean, seeded Number 1, had committed herself to participate in the tournament, despite the Riggs match. She planned to take Thursday night off in order to play in the Astrodome. Now, she was about to play in the first round. If she won, she would immediately retake the court to play the second round, then wait until Friday, after the Riggs match, to rejoin the tournament in the quarterfinals.

Tickets for any seat at the first round at the Net-Set, an outdoor complex of composition-surface courts nestled within a new ring of condominium apartments, cost $3 as compared with $100 for a ringside seat in the Astrodome. Yet only a few hundred spectators turned out in the hazy early fall Texas sunlight to catch King in action.

The scene was typical of the languid first days of a normal women's pro tournament, except for the fact that the Net-Set was crawling with reporters (who almost outnumbered the spectators) anxious to interview the star after she played. She had been so aloof no one dared miss the opportunity to talk to her, nor to see whether her physical condition was as grave as they had been led to believe.

She took the match easily, 6-0, 6-4, while her secretary,

Marilyn Barnett, sat next to me in the stands assuring me that Vitamin E and Three Musketeers candy bars had helped bring Billie Jean back to full strength.

"I feel wonderful," she said calmly at the press conference. "I did *not* have cancer, hepatitis or hypoglycemia. I wasn't on my deathbed. *You* people," she said accusingly, "invented all that."

It was not quite true—her husband, Larry, among others, had been the source of the hypoglycemia reports. Nevertheless, she did look fit enough, and she was in what I had come to know as her basic, manic fighting mood.

When someone asked what she had thought of Bobby's recent pronouncements, she grinned. "The one thing that really got me was when he said he'd jump off the Pasadena suicide bridge if he lost," she replied with a gleam in her eye. It was still there when another reporter asked about rumors that she had withered under the pressure of preparing for the biggest prize ever offered for a tennis exhibition.

"I don't think he's ever played a $100,000 match either," she shot back. "We'll see Thursday who can take the pressure and who can't!"

It almost sounded like the old Billie Jean again. Or was it?

With a glance, she took in the television cameras in the back of the room, the mass of print reporters seated in front of them, the radio reporters' Sonys mounted in a row on the table at which she was seated. "You know," she said, "women's tennis started right here in Houston three years ago. But we never had press conferences like this. We never *had* press conferences, period."

The historical coincidences of Houston, tennis and women seemed quite striking that week, for indeed, the growth of the women's movement in three years had paralleled the growth of women's tennis.

In August, 1970, thousands of women had literally or figuratively gone on strike to celebrate the New Feminism's first women's rights day. The same month, two women tennis pros, Ceci Martinez and Esme Emanuel, dissatisfied like so many of their colleagues with the lower prize money awarded women in comparison to men at major tournaments, had circulated a questionnaire on the issue among fans attending the U. S. Open at Forest Hills. The seeds for a separate, independent women's pro tennis tour had been sown; a month later, the first sprouts pushed their way up to the surface—in Houston.

The women had expressed outrage at the prize money being offered that month by promoter Jack Kramer at the Pacific Southwest Championships, held each year in California. The ratio was $12,500 for the men, $1,500 for the women. Spurred on by Billie Jean, a group of the women threatened to boycott the tournament unless Kramer came up with a more equal distribution. When he refused, eight of them signed contracts for a symbolic $1 each with Gladys Heldman, a Houston resident who was the publisher of *World Tennis* magazine. Heldman, a dynamic businesswoman who was to become a prime mover in the women's tennis world, then set up the first all-women's pro tournament at the Houston Racquet Club. She persuaded Joseph Cullman, head of Philip Morris, to put up sponsorship money on behalf of Virginia Slims, the cigarette whose ad campaign had drawn the fire of feminists for the word "baby" at the end of its slogan. Total prize at the Houston tournament was $7,500. The first prize of $1,600 was won by Rosemary Casals. The New Feminism in tennis was born.

In 1971, the Slims, as the tour and its players were becoming known, held tournaments in nineteen cities with a total of $309,100 in the prize money kitty. In 1972, one more city was added and the kitty swelled to $501,275. The 1973 figures were twenty-two cities, $775,000 in prizes. By comparison, World Championship Tennis, the men's pro circuit, played in twenty-four cities during the year for $1,280,000.

In pro baseball, football or basketball terms, women's tennis was still a baby, but in terms of its development as a big league sport, it had come a long way.

Like a racquet-bearing Wonder Woman leading the

Amazons, Billie Jean had spearheaded the equal rights movement in tennis. She had been one of the first four players to sign professional tour contracts in 1968, the ringleader behind the rebellion against Kramer, the union organizer who had locked sixty-three women in a conference room at Wimbledon in June, 1973, in order to hammer out a Women's Tennis Association that would speak for the players' interests in tournament and television rights negotiations, the agitator who had needled the U. S. Open into finally boosting the women's prize money so it would be equal to the men's.

In the course of her decade as the co-champion of international women's tennis (she shared the crown with Margaret Court, in most experts' estimations) she had earned fourteen Wimbledon titles and a reputation as a big mouth to go with it. While Margaret hid, as it were, behind her husband's skirts, Billie Jean crisscrossed the country tirelessly promoting herself, women's tennis and women's rights. She spoke to youth groups. She played exhibitions for the Women's Political Caucus. She signed a manifesto in favor of abortion, acknowledging she had had one.

She was, I thought, listening to her at the Net-Set Racquet Club that afternoon, the epitome of what some men found so threatening about the women's movement. It was poetic justice that she, not Margaret, play in the Astrodome for $100,000. If Billie Jean King didn't exist, Bobby Riggs would have had to invent her.

Billie Jean had played one match, taken a shower, changed her dress, come back out on the court an hour later and beaten Kristien Kemmer 6-0, 6-2. "Hypoglycemia like that we should all have," said a Houston matron sitting next to me. I started thinking again about the $500 bet and my fall jacket.

There were only three people on line Tuesday at one of the Astrodome box offices that were studded on the fringes of the parking lot. "The $100 seats are almost gone," explained Sidney Shlenker, the boss of the Astrodome, "but most of the $6 ones are still left." He shrugged. "Everybody knows you won't be able to see from all the way up there." Besides, ticket sales had dropped to near zero after Billie Jean had defaulted at the U. S. Open three weeks earlier, he added. Nevertheless, both Shlenker and Jerry Perenchio, the promoter whose previous claim to fame had been packaging the Ali-Frazier fight, expected to have 35,000 people in the stands (the capacity of the Dome in its baseball configuration was 46,000) when the match, blacked out on local television, got under way Thursday night.

Bobby Riggs was doing his best to sell tickets. While Billie Jean camped out in her suite at the posh Houston Oaks Hotel a few miles from the Dome area with her parents, her husband, her secretary, her coach and a handful of other close associates, Riggs roamed the lobby of the Astroworld Hotel across the street from the arena making friends and giving lengthy interviews to everyone from Howard Cosell to the sports editor of the Fondren High School newspaper.

Bobby had been in town for a week, playing nightly exhibitions in the bubble. It had been specially constructed and equipped with a Sportface-carpeted court to give both players a practice area similar to what they would be working out on in the Dome itself. (The stadium, with its zippered strips of plastic grass called Astroturf, would remain in its baseball diamond layout until after the Wednesday doubleheader. Then the workmen would lay out a basketball-like wooden platform stretching from first to third base over the mound, cement Sportface carpeting over it, and set up the "ringside" rows of folding chairs on all four sides to create the tennis court.)

"I haven't met a man yet who didn't want me to win," Bobby said with a pleasant smile into a microphone as dozens of fans crowded around him in the bubble Tuesday night following his workout.

The crowd didn't seem to bother him; on the contrary, he looked as contented as a little boy in a zoo. It was hard to believe this runty, genial man with the Mickey Rooney face was fifty-five years old. His hair was a bright reddish brown (courtesy of Clairol), his body trim. Only the soft folds of skin at the neck and his deafness (he was too vain to wear a hearing aid) betrayed his age. Behind him hovered a pop-eyed man with rippling muscles carrying a small white bag: Rheo Blair, Riggs's nutritionist, who had a theory about vitamins as a cure for schizophrenia. The bag was filled with brown bottles of every vitamin invented plus several not yet named. He slipped Bobby a few calcium pills which Riggs nonchalantly swallowed in between questions.

When the interviews were all finished, Bobby started to leave. Suddenly he turned to the reporters still standing around, and, with a smile, pulled off the white crew neck sweater he was wearing. Underneath was a blue tennis shirt with holes cut out around the nipples. "I was gonna give this to Billie Jean King—she might look better in it than I would," he said, smiling benignly.

That night, after dinner, Jerry Perenchio took Bobby and a group of reporters on a tour of his penthouse suite at the Astroworld, in which each bedroom was decorated in a different style. The place suggested Bloomingdale's Barbara D'Arcy model rooms designed on an acid trip: the Tarzan room featured a leopardskin tissue box, the Fu Manchu room a Chinese symbol above the toilet that Perenchio swore translated as "Please flush." Afterwards, Bobby insisted on inviting us to his own, more humble suite, where cartons loaded with copies of his autobiography, *Court Hustler,* were stacked along one wall, and cartons of Hai Karate, a cologne he had done commercials for, were stacked along the other. I opened the refrigerator door in the bar and an avalanche of avocados came rumbling out. ("Bobby's on a regime of small feedings," Rheo told me.) Everywhere I looked there were paper plates heaped with vitamins. Bobby periodically gobbled handfuls, offering the plates to his guests as if they were M-and-M's.

It was one o'clock in the morning, two nights before

the match, and yet the Bobby Riggs mouth seemed to have a life of its own. I couldn't help liking him—he was funny, astute in his tennis conversation, and remarkably candid now that the microphones had disappeared.

"On the court, she's like greased lightning," he said of Billie Jean. "She makes me look like I'm in slow motion. I haven't played three out of five sets since 1950; I'll be lucky to get through three." It almost sounded as though he had a premonition. But when I finally asked why he was the prohibitive favorite, he said with an old vaudevillian's assurance: "This is my cup of tea, my dish, this pressure, this circus stuff.

"I don't believe," he continued, quite seriously, "that she's as stable as I am with the eyes of the world on us."

Someone wanted to know how much he'd been able to hustle up in side bets since arriving in Houston. He snorted. "You kidding? I can't find a dime's worth of King money in town."

I was having second thoughts about my fall jacket again. I was also having second thoughts about Billie Jean and women's tennis. I had been following the game closely all year. Despite my conviction that a King loss would prove nothing, I knew that in the eyes of a skeptical public, a Riggs victory would somehow confirm Bobby's bleatings about women being inferior athletes.

I was sure that wasn't true. I had watched too many wonderfully coordinated women play too many exciting matches.

But there was something else I was not sure of. In the clutch, when the chips were really down, could the Old Lady hang tough? Could any woman jock? They were questions that had been tugging at my consciousness all year long.

31

Philadelphia

Max-Pax

"THIS IS A BUSINESS NOW," TORY FRETZ WAS SAYING. "IT'S not like seven years ago when you went out on some country club court all in white, you won a tournament, you got a trophy and that was it."

We were sitting in the Palestra, a drafty old basketball arena on the University of Pennsylvania campus where Virginia Slims was holding its tenth in a series of weekly tournaments during the winter-spring season. Tory, a tall, slim woman with a blonde shag and startling tinted contact lenses the color of the Caribbean, was an old pro of thirty who was explaining to me how much women's tennis had changed since the bad old days when players got paid with a "green handshake" and everyone was called an amateur.

"We never used to have crowds like this," Tory continued, waving a hand at the 3,500 people who filled perhaps two thirds of the hard wooden seats that framed the court, a green carpet called Sportface laid down over the basketball floor. "And the purses! Top prize here is $12,000. In 1967, I was Number 4 in the country and I made $50 a week under the table. I paid for my airfare and that was about it."

To me, the entire look of the place was immediately impressive. Not the size of the crowd, which seemed small compared to what a college basketball game might draw, not even the prize money. But the trimmings were thoroughly professional. On Friday night, when the quarterfinal round was played (the tournament had begun on Wednesday with a sixteen-player draw; the semis were to be Saturday night, the final Sunday afternoon), models were handing out sample packets of Virginia Slims cigarettes at the entrances, hawkers were selling a slickly produced fifty-eight-page program called "Lob!," Max-Pax coffee cans filled with fresh flowers decorated tables in a makeshift snack bar and a full complement of Philadelphia and New York sportswriters were on hand to record the action. On court, Rosemary Casals, the Number 7 player in the world, was delighting the crowd with her usual furious, scrambling style against Janet Newberry, a nineteen-year-old who was the fastest rising star in the women's game. Everything seemed to be in order.

It would be hard for a spectator to know how shaky the finances of this seemingly professional tournament really were. The proceeds were to go to underprivileged children. General Foods, one of several companies that were just starting to sponsor women's tennis as a promotional outlet (the firm's ads featured Nancy Richey Gunter holding a coffee cup, looking as if she had just stepped out of a television soap opera), was putting up the $50,000 prize money. In exchange, it got the coffee can decorations on the tables and the Max-Pax brand name on the tournament. Thus, just as some tournaments were "Virginia Slims," "S & H Green Stamps" and "Fabergé" championships, this was officially the "Max-Pax Coffee Tennis Classic," which somehow made me think of coffee-colored tennis balls. The tournament was being run by Marilyn and Ed Fernberger, a bustling husband and wife team, well known in tennis circles, who also ran the men's pro tennis tournaments held each year in Philadelphia's big sports arena, the Spectrum. This was the first time a women's pro tour had played in town, and Marilyn Fernberger was not at all happy with the results. Tory Fretz and the other players viewed tournaments from the perspective of how far they had progressed since amateur days. Mrs. Fernberger, on the other hand, focused on how far they still had to go to catch up with other professional sports, even men's tennis.

"You won't find a slicker promotion than Virginia Slims does anywhere," she said that evening in a tiny room beneath the stands that served as office, storage room and secret cooler for beer (not allowed for sale inside the Palestra). "But it can't stop with beautiful colored stationery and cigarettes handed out at the door." The tournament, it seemed, cost $105,000, including prize money, to run, but only two thirds of that came from gate receipts, with the rest coming from General Foods. "No sport is totally professional until the gate supports it," declared Mrs. Fernberger, a former club player who comes on like a modern Philadelphia suburban version of Rosalind Russell. "And so far women's tennis has been totally subsidized. As a divided group, the women don't draw," she said with annoyance.

She was referring to the breach between the Virginia Slims tour group and the United States Lawn Tennis Association's rival circuit. The U.S.L.T.A. was the official governing body of organized tennis in this country, just as its sister organizations were in other countries. The U.S.L.T.A. was run by amateurs—wealthy tennis lovers who were not professional sports administrators.

When the Slims group started its own professional tour, it defied the authority of the U.S.L.T.A. by refusing to pay "sanction fees"—percentages of the receipts. (The association would, in return, give its okay to the Slims circuit.) The U.S.L.T.A. also objected to the contracts the players had signed with Gladys Heldman. A similar battle had been fought between the U.S.L.T.A. and the men's pro group, World Championship Tennis.

By the end of 1972, the Slims and the U.S.L.T.A. were locked in a bitter feud. The U.S.L.T.A. threatened to have the Slims women banned from international championships such as Wimbledon and Forest Hills. In January, 1973, the Slims retaliated with a lawsuit charging an "illegal trade boycott."

The upshot was that as 1973 began, the Slims—with

sixty-four of the world's best players—began its "unsanctioned" spring circuit of thirteen tournaments throughout the United States, each one with a minimum of $25,000 total prize money. The U.S.L.T.A., meanwhile, hastily organized its own eight-week competing tour with tournaments featuring a minimum of $20,000 prize money. The U.S.L.T.A.'s big drawing cards were Chris Evert and Evonne Goolagong, who, fearful of being banned from Wimbledon, had elected to join the new group. There was also a feeling among tennis observers that the men who managed Evonne and Chris felt their clients would be subjected to less competition and an easier schedule on the shorter tour.

The feud was another skirmish in tennis's perpetual war between progressives and traditionalists. To a tennis outsider, the war had about as much interest as a War of the Roses textbook does to a botany student. But the main point was that for most of 1973 it split the leading younger attractions in women's tennis—Chris and Evonne—away from the larger Slims group, which had most of the established stars including Margaret Court and Billie Jean King. For Mrs. Fernberger, the split was a convenient jumping-off point for complaints about the women themselves.

"The top eight, twelve players are professional in their attitude," she said. "After that, they don't grasp what it's all about. They don't know from PR. Last Sunday one qualifier had been set up with a reporter for an interview. She sat down with him for ten minutes, and suddenly jumped up and left—a friend of hers from college was in town and she wanted to see her!" Mrs. Fernberger drew on her Virginia Slim and cast an Auntie Mame glance at the ceiling. "It's a carryover from the juniors, from amateur days. For so many of them, it's just like they're going out to have a good hit. Well, having a hit is not the same as the approach you're supposed to take to professional sports."

Right. I was as intrigued by Mrs. Fernberger's phrasing as I was by what she was saying. "Having a hit." "Juniors." Tennis, I learned, had a whole special vocabulary.

"Juniors" meant the amateur circuit, in which young boys and girls work their way up through the different age groups—"under twelve," "under fourteen" and so on, before they try their luck at "women's" or "men's" tennis. The juniors are part of the minor leagues of tennis, the place where kids get the feel of competition, where anxious parents coach from the sidelines the way they do at Little League games, where many a fine prospect is buried under the weight of too much pressure at too early an age.

"Having a hit" meant either practicing, or having a fun game with someone. It became notorious later in the spring when, after losing to Bobby Riggs, Margaret Court said she had merely expected to have "a bit of a Sunday hit" with him.

Then there were even more esoteric phrases, like "hitting through the ball," "getting pace on the ball" and "hitting out." All three meant getting more oomph on the ball, although the first few times I heard them I couldn't imagine why anyone would want to hit the ball "out" when she could hit it "in."

Finally, there was the scoring shorthand—"I beat her 3 and 4," meaning a score of 6-3, 6-4. I loved these new phrases; they reminded me of how great it felt the first time I yelled "Copy!" in a newsroom or an editor told me to "Boil it down to a D-head." It was like breaking a code, or learning a password. When I first brought myself to say "3 and love" I felt as though I had been a tennis insider all my life.

"Having a good hit. . . ." Just as Marilyn and I were talking, the quarterfinal match between Rosemary Casals and Janet Newberry ended, with Casals the winner in three sets. Rosie was ushered into the "interview room"—a locker room next to the office—for another tennis ritual, the post-match press conference. Most of the players disliked these interviews with good reason. As if by rote, match after match, reporters would ask the same tired questions: "What was the turning point? What's your previous record against her?" while the player would sit there, exhausted, dreaming about a hot shower. It was no different here. Asked what her record was against Margaret Court, her next opponent, Rosie explained that she had lost to the Australian in the past five outings. But she had almost beaten Court, she added, at Forest Hills the previous summer: "I had her 5-2 in the third. . . ." It was a phrase that would echo, from tournament to tournament, like an *ostinato* of missed opportunities.

Sometimes it was "4-1," sometimes "5-3." But the voice would always trail off, as the player relived defeat snatched from the jaws of near-victory. For certain players, and Rosie Casals was one of them, "5-2 in the third" was often the closest they came to first-prize money.

While the matches were going on, the players who weren't on the court sat in clumps in the stands, kibitzing, everyone in well-tailored slacks and sharp, expensive sweaters, a few with suede jackets. Karen Krantzcke, a 6-foot-1-inch Australian player with the stooped shoulders of someone who is always ducking low door lintels, sat calmly doing needlepoint. Francoise Durr, the longtime French star, just sat, a Gallic pout on her lips, her pale face made garish by too much green eye shadow, a victim of hepatitis earlier in the year who was still suffering the after-effects. Barry Court, Margaret's husband, sat in a box seat during his wife's match with Valerie Ziegenfuss, watching each move intently in between sips from a can of the forbidden beer. After Ziegenfuss lost, she bumped into Barry on her way out of the arena. "You didn't do your job last night—she was too full of energy," Val told him in a mock-chiding tone.

The majority of the players ate dinner in the university's training house a few minutes' walk away. As part of their arrangements for the tournament, they had been given meal chits, and the food at the training house was rated good. Much to my surprise, many of the players also received free lodging. A legacy from amateur days, the traditional lodging was in the home of wealthy or ambitious tennis club members, although sometimes, in a new city, players found themselves offered little more than a cot in the basement next to the washing machine. (On rare occasions, they were offered accommodations even more bizarre. One player found herself in the home of a lonely widow who expected her to share the only bedroom's double bed with her. The player slept on the floor.) In the vocabulary of the players, spending the week in the spare room of someone's private house was "staying with people," as opposed to booking a hotel room. "It used to be that families would bid for the stars," one player told me. "You know, a status thing. They would say, especially of the men, 'If I can't have the Aussies, I don't want anybody.' " With the increasing prize money, the leading players had begun to forsake the home cooking and occasional forced chummi- ness of "staying with people," so that in Philadelphia at least half a dozen were staying at the Penn Center Inn in town. Even there, they had a special deal—$10 a night players' rate. At the time, it struck me as odd, these profes- sional athletes bunking for the week in somebody's den. (I couldn't imagine the Mets, for example, doing such a thing on road trips.) But later I could see that it might be an attractive alternative to weeks of faceless Holiday Inns.

That night, after the matches, an incident that sym- bolized women's tennis stayed with me. It had been dur- ing the Ziegenfuss-Court match. Val, a powerfully built but feminine twenty-three-year-old with a bit of a ferret face, was getting demolished by Court, who had so domi- nated the circuit in previous weeks the players were joking about kidnapping her son in order to distract her. After losing the first seven games of the match, Val managed to eke out a game (her only one of the night, it turned out) when Margaret netted a few easy shots. When the umpire announced "Game, Miss Ziegenfuss," the crowd applauded loudly.

Val looked up at the stands, smiled painfully, and made a self-deprecating curtsy.

The matches Saturday did not start until evening, but, from 10 A.M. on, the players drifted in and out of the Palestra to practice, meet with business associates or just pass the time. Because there was only one court, the players had signed up for hour-long practice periods the night before on a schedule posted by Peachy Kellmeyer, the tour director. One hour on the schedule had Barry Court penciled in for a hit with Ed Fernberger.

Tory Fretz had come in early to get some heat treatment on an elbow that was giving her trouble. "That's another big difference from the old days," she said. "This tournament, we have a real trainer, which we've never had before. We need somebody like that to travel with us all the time. We don't know how to take care of ourselves."

The trainer, "Big Al" Marchfeld, was actually a small-time jewelry manufacturer who had become a masseur as a way of getting close to sports, the real love of his life. A hulking but gentle New Yorker, he worked part-time as a scorekeeper for the Knicks, doing rubdowns on the side. He had acted as trainer at several previous men's and women's tournaments and had been hired for the week in Philadelphia by the Fernbergers.

Most of the women agreed with Tory that a trainer was a fine idea. Big Al, who was enjoying sudden fame as an expert on women's ailments (the Philadelphia sportswriters had all interviewed him about nudity in the locker room), was greatly in favor of it himself. "The girls seem to think that mother nature is the only healer. The men are so much more conscious of physical fitness. If they need a rubdown for a muscle pull, they'll get a rubdown. The men will always relax, maybe close their eyes for a few minutes before a match. The women, they'll be sitting in the stands, chatting. When I brought this up to the girls the past few days, they said they'd never thought about it before! I think," he declared, "it's about time the women had a trainer to stand over them with a stick." (Neither the Slims nor the U.S.L.T.A. tour ever did hire a permanent trainer, although there were massages available from local people at many of the tour stops.)

The main ailments among the women, Marchfeld continued, were the same as those among the men: tennis elbow, pulled muscles, stiff necks. Women did suffer more back trouble, though, a rare complaint among the men. "The big problem is, the girls are too lazy to look into treatment."

Big Al took a proprietary attitude toward his clients. That night, he and Tory watched from the stands as Wendy Overton and Karen Krantzcke played doubles against Margaret Court and Lesley Hunt. Both Overton and Hunt had used Marchfeld's services earlier, Wendy for a pulled muscle in her arm, Hunt for a sore back. "Well, Al, your two patients are out there," Tory remarked.

"One bad arm, one bad back . . . some stiff necks, a bad leg—I'm gonna send out to Johns Hopkins for some spare limbs, see if we can get them in time for next week's tournament!" He laughed. When Lesley Hunt got to the semifinals in the singles, Big Al was so excited you'd have thought he had played her matches himself.

There was a loose, jocular atmosphere around the court during the practice sessions. The women played in T-shirts and shorts, a few in handsome double-knit warm-up outfits similar to track suits. When Ziegenfuss, now out of the tournament, sent a beautiful backhand sizzling past Hunt, she let out a whistle, then cried, "I wish I was in the middle of a match!" When Hunt, who faced Kerry Harris in a semifinal, waved good-bye to a friend at the end of the hour, he yelled out, ". . . and wish Kerry luck for me." Hunt replied by giving him a good-natured finger in the air.

Later in the afternoon, I had a talk with Wendy Overton, one of the players who had been lured back into competitive tennis by the growing prize money. At twenty-six, she was, as one writer put it, the kind of girl who inspired the Beach Boys' song "Wendy." Long-legged, pug-nosed, her sun-bleached straight hair falling midway down her back, she was a prime exception to the rule (as laid down by male tennis buffs) that the best-looking women in tennis were in the stands rather than on the court. Another Floridian—roughly 80 percent of the American players were natives or residents of either Florida or California—

she had graduated from Rollins College, then worked as a secretary and tennis teacher until 1972, when she joined the Slims. With her strong serve and volley game, she became an overnight sensation, winning $23,350 in her first year on the tour.

"When I went to college, it wasn't within the realm of possibility to make a living as a touring pro," she said. "My dad wasn't about to subsidize me, so it was only after I saw you could make money here that I quit my job. I mean, my parents were all for me as the all-American girl, but that meant it was okay to play tournaments during the summer in between semesters. This was a great opportunity for me."

But Wendy was beginning to experience a "sophomore jinx." She had arm trouble—"I took off a week and when I came back it was like I was a beginner; couldn't hit a thing!"—and, worse, "psyching" trouble. When I asked about the thrill of winning, Wendy wrinkled her nose the way she did so often on the court when she was concentrating hard. "I haven't been there yet. I've never won a major tournament," she said slowly. "I'm close, I know I'm close. But I must realize they're beatable—Margaret, Rosie, Billie Jean. Until I realize that"—she sighed—"I have a psychological disease."

The Arm

"Look at her arms," Peachy Kellmeyer had whispered the night before as we watched Margaret Court play in the quarterfinal against Ziegenfuss. Indeed, as she crouched at the baseline waiting for a serve, the arms of the Australian whom the players called "Big Maggie" and the sportswriters called "Big Mama" seemed to hang halfway to her knees, the long, bony fingers wrapped around the racquet handle in a vise-like grip. Rosie Casals, her semifinal opponent, had nicknamed her The Arm, because, said Rosie, when Margaret came to the net all you saw was that big right one reaching in every direction as if it were infinitely stretchable elastic.

The London Human Biomechanics Laboratory once tested Court and found that not only were her arms more than three inches longer than the normal woman's, but that her right-hand grip strength was 121½ pounds—as strong as many male college athletes. Now, as she sat with me in the stands just before practice, the same hand was busy throwing a tennis ball to little Danny Court, who was crawling around on the sidelines.

For the first four months of the circuit, Margaret had totally dominated the Slims—winning seven out of the nine tournaments so far. (Billie Jean King, her decade-long rival, had been ill and played only four of the tournaments.)

When she played Margaret was one of the women

whose image seemed to transform itself from minute to minute. In motion she was the consummate athlete who leaped at balls like an orangutan, or more humanly, like a rangy basketball forward. But as soon as a point was over, another image would immediately resurface. She would straighten her shoulders, raise her head as if an invisible crown were being placed on it, stare straight ahead and walk slowly, regally, back to position. You could almost hear "Pomp and Circumstance." Margaret Court carried herself like a queen, and spectators who complained that she didn't look feminine enough were missing the other half of her on-court persona.

Here, close up, the first impression she gave was of being considerably older than her thirty years. A great many of the players did appear older than they were—the sun, the squint of intense concentration day after day, the showers that dried out the skin took their toll in deep lines about the eyes and mouth. Lesley Hunt had the beginnings of them at twenty-two; Margaret, after eleven years on the tournament circuit, had more than her share. Yet the light-blue, double-lidded eyes were friendly, the rawboned leatheriness of the freckled arms and fingers were feminized by a diamond ring and wedding ring on the left hand, the neck softened by a cross on a chain. Even in a warm-up suit, there was nothing masculine about her. She was very much a lady.

We were talking about traveling with Danny and the problems it posed. The Courts' entourage included no baby-sitter, she said, because both she and Barry liked to be with Danny as much as possible. As always, they were "staying with people"—in this case, a family she had met a few years back on a previous visit to Philadelphia—because it was "much easier, foodwise, washing, all that sort of thing."

She had an odd, high-pitched voice, with the distinctive Australian accent that sounds to American ears like a composite of English and Texan. It had a singsong quality to it, just as her answers to basic questions did—they were

46

trite, pat phrases obviously recycled many times in years of interviews. "We enjoy staying in a home," she recited. "We enjoy being with people. Barry enjoys meeting people very much and I think we've made a lot of friends throughout the country. We go back and stay with them quite often."

So much for staying with people. I asked about plans for the future. "I enjoy the game. I enjoyed it when I was sixteen and I enjoy it now. I just hope I'll enjoy it the rest of my life. I like to teach and I'll probably do some of that when I stop touring. I feel when somebody's been gifted with something, you should give it back, help others, show others, give other people pleasure."

So much for the future. Run, Dick, Run.

The Margaret Court story was in fact more interesting than Margaret Court, the person, for the simple reason that she was among the very greatest athletes of either sex Australia had produced. The daughter of a factory foreman, Margaret grew up in Albury, a small town in New South Wales. As a child, she and friends would sneak onto a private tennis court to play the national game when the club members weren't looking. (Neither of her parents were tennis players.) She later claimed that she learned to volley as well as she did because she was forced to play the net all the time by her friends, to prevent the ball from bouncing out of the court where it would have been detected by club members.

Margaret was apparently such a fine athlete that she had no trouble switching as a child from being a southpaw (she still signed autographs with her left hand) to a right-hander. She was so fast as a girl that one coach tried to persuade her to give up tennis and concentrate on the 440 and 880 dashes instead. She was such a quick student that by seventeen she had become the youngest woman ever to win the Australian Championship. By nineteen, she was ranked Number 1 in the world. She remained at or near the top for the next decade, despite a year's retirement, marriage and a family.

Throughout her career, Margaret had been a nut on physical fitness. Other women might consider lifting weights unfeminine, but Margaret had done it and could hoist 150 pounds. When she wasn't on the road, she did roadwork and skipped rope to keep in shape.

In June, 1971, at Wimbledon, the renowned Court coordination inexplicably went awry. "My legs were going one way and my arms were going the other way. I didn't know why!" She laughed. "Then I found out I was pregnant."

Court retired from the circuit right after Wimbledon, but played tennis socially a few times a week until she was in her eighth month. When Danny was born, she nursed him for three months, playing no tennis at all. After that came a single month of practice before she rejoined the circuit. She promptly won her first tournament. "You know," she mused, "the doctors say it helps a woman, a pregnancy. I know a lot of runners have run better times after giving birth than they ever did in their lives. Whether it's made me stronger, I don't know. But when I quit once before, in '66, I was only twenty-four, and it took me twelve full months to get back into the game. This time, it took no time at all. But I was lighter after having Danny than before I started—eight pounds lighter—and right now I'm lighter than I've ever been in my life."

Remarkable as her physical comeback was, Margaret said that the biggest change in her, after Danny's birth, was not physical but mental. "I used to be very tense," she said quietly. "I find I don't worry about tennis anywhere near as much as I used to. I don't have the time now. I have a family."

There was no doubt in my mind then that she meant what she said, yet future events were to suggest that Margaret was a far more complex and contradictory person than she let on. Despite her fifty major world titles, despite her utter mastery of the Slims circuit, Margaret was regarded by insiders as a choke artist, who either froze or

got leg cramps at tense moments in a match, both supposedly a sign of "nerves."

In Philadelphia, in April, she was telling the world
that having a baby had helped rid her of her nervousness.
In Ramona, California, on a Mother's Day in May, she
contracted nerves at the worst possible time, serving up a
$10,000 check to Bobby Riggs on a silver platter in the first
mixed-singles match in tennis, a match that would haunt
her the rest of the year.

This afternoon the Riggs match seemed like the least
important thing on her mind. "I think it's probably good
for women's tennis," she responded singsong to a question
about it. "I think he's been a little bit too outspoken about
women having an inferior game. I'd like to prove a point.
I know—everybody knows—that I couldn't touch the top
forty men in the world. But none of them is Bobby Riggs."

The point, she emphasized, was that to most spectators
who were themselves weekend tennis players, women's
tennis was much more fun to watch than the Slam! Serve!
Crunch! Volley! game the men played. Thus, she argued,
in terms of attracting fans, of helping them learn to play
their own strokes better, women's tennis was superior to
that of the men. In turn, women's tennis had encouraged
spectators to go out and hit more, boosting the growth of
recreational tennis across the country. "Everybody here is
playing the game," Margaret said. "I mean look at the
courts outside." (There were a dozen college courts in front
of the Palestra.) "They're packed from five o'clock in the
morning practically. People here are so willing to learn,
whether they're ten years old or sixty."

The same point was made to me by Gladys Heldman,
the driving force behind the Slims tour. "If women play
more consistently, have more shots, and men can learn
from them, why shouldn't they make as much or more prize
money than the men?"

Bobby Riggs, nickel-and-diming it in men's seniors,
had decided to get himself a piece of that increasingly rich

action in the women's game. But for Margaret, in April, the Riggs match was going to be a small interruption in what she hoped would be a triumphal march to her second Grand Slam.* When I asked if she had planned any special preparation for the Mother's Day match, she shrugged. "Nah, not particularly. He doesn't hit the ball that hard anymore."

Only once, when I turned the conversation to money, did Court get a real edge in her voice. She was going for the Grand Slam, she said, because she "liked to have challenge." What about prize money? I asked. What about winning more than the $100,000-plus Billie Jean had won the year before?

"Once I start thinking about the money I'm playing for, I think I might as well give the game up," she said, her jaw set. "Because it's never been me, and why change now?"

Wasn't prize money an important manifestation of the new professionalism in the game? I asked.

"Well, I can't help it," she snapped. Then, calmly: "I think it's done a lot for the game. But I've been through both sides, amateur and pro. Now kids seem to think, well, it's a pretty easy way of making a living." She looked hurt, as if remembering how much fun it had been playing matches for under-the-table expense money and shiny trophies. "Just because there's money in the game shouldn't change your attitude. This is where so many young people coming into the game today . . . that's all they're going to know is money. I think this is really missing out. When they're finished with tennis they'll probably be bitter against it, because they won't have had any fun out of it."

I shut off my tape recorder and she jumped off the bench to grab Danny, who was about to wander off into the Palestra's corridors. Was she having any fun? I wondered. Chris Evert admired Margaret, but once said, "It must be lonely being Number 1." The other players—par-

---

* A "Grand Slam" means winning the four major titles—the Australian, French, Wimbledon and United States Open singles championships—in a single year.

ticularly the other Australians—complained that Margaret was aloof from the rest of the tour group, hurrying away from the tournament site with Barry every night, moving from city to city within her own self-contained family circle. They said the Courts stayed with people not because it was convenient, but because it was cheap. They said, without putting it quite so bluntly, that Margaret's disdain for the dollar was phony, that after more than a decade collecting trophies she was out this year to get *her* piece of the action at last. Why else, they asked, was she here, after having won just about every tournament that counted on this planet? I made no judgments. But by the end of the year, Margaret had played eighteen and won fourteen out of twenty-three Slims tournaments as well as a slew of others in Europe, the United States and Australia, had sustained four injuries (torn muscle, leg cramps, flu and penicillin reaction) that disabled her during matches and had picked up a whopping $205,000 in the process. Whether for love or money, it was an impressive performance.

But even though she was a great champion, Margaret did not impress me as a person that day in Philadelphia. Her reticence, her blandness annoyed me even though I understood that much of it was due to a basically shy, introverted nature. You are dull, Margaret Court, I said silently as she played her practice session. One day later in the year I mentioned to a tennis official that Margaret lacked one of the most common mannerisms among the women players: she never talked to herself during a match. "What," he replied coolly, "could she possibly think of to say?"

Rosebud

AT 5 FEET 2¼ INCHES, ROSEBUD, AS MARGARET COURT affectionately called Rosemary Casals, was among the smallest women in pro tennis, a factor always cited by reporters as one reason why she just missed being one of the great players of all time. (Margaret was amused by the nickname Casals had given her: "She may call me The Arm, but she gets around the court pretty well, too. She's built so close to the ground, you know.") Rosie was also among the most powerful and the most acrobatic, with an overhead that could take the cover off a ball and a few flat-on-the-floor and behind-the-back shots that hadn't been named yet.

For practice Saturday afternoon, Rosie wore one of her typically conservative outfits: a psychedelic-orange satin warm-up suit with black stripes down the arms and legs that made her look like a member of some peewee basketball team. During a match, she usually looked more like an Apache brave on the warpath, with a bright pink or blue bandana keeping the jet-black hair off her high-cheekboned face, her dark eyes fierce with concentration. When she climbed an invisible ladder to reach for a lob, her Spalding Speedshaft would club down on the ball like a tomahawk.

Rosie was, more than anything else, the classic rebel, the pugnacious outcast from the wrong side of the tracks who carved out a life for herself in tennis battling the authorities, as well as her opponents, every step of the way. Like Pancho Gonzales years before her, she outraged the Brahmins because she brought color and charisma, fire and fury to a sport that ladies and gentlemen were in the habit of applauding politely. You didn't applaud a Rosie Casals, you cheered her until your throat got hoarse, because that's what her game was all about. Even more than Billie Jean, Rosie brought gut-clutching excitement to the women's game, an excitement that was the natural extension of her personality.

Her father had been born in San Salvador before migrating to San Francisco, where Rosie grew up, skipping school half the time to hit tennis balls with anyone in Golden Gate Park who would give her a game. She barely graduated from high school, leaving a month before the term ended (with the principal's permission) to play Wimbledon. Now at only twenty-four, she had been playing big league women's tennis for a decade.

If ever there were the ultimate female jock, I assumed, it would be Rosie. I couldn't have been more wrong. Rosie might not have loved school, but she read Hesse in her hotel room. (Chris Evert, in contrast, read movie magazines and *I'm OK, You're OK,* the best-seller among tennis players in 1972. Billie Jean King read *Sports Illustrated* and Herman Wouk.)

While most of the players ate quiet meals and spent their evenings doing laundry, Rosie always had a full cultural schedule—rock concerts and palmists, the theater in London and New York, the Grand Old Opry in Nashville. She was a shrewd analyst of the game and its politics, a fluent conversationalist even if too many of her sentences began with "Whereas" or "In respect to" when she was struggling to sound educated.

She could also be thoroughly, refreshingly crude about things she hated, among them linesmen who made bad calls, Bobby Riggs and the United States Lawn Tennis Association.

In one match played for the benefit of a corrective

vision charity, Rosie spat at a linesman who had made several errors, "Where did they get you, from the eye bank?"

Asked about Riggs's ability long before she was hired to do the TV color commentary on the Astrodome match—a commentary delivered in Casals' typically blunt style that infuriated many viewers—Rosie said succinctly, "He's an old has-been who can't see, he can't hear, he walks like a duck and he's an idiot besides."

When I asked about the U.S.L.T.A., which had once suspended her for turning professional, she retorted, "I'd like to plant a bomb in their office, call them all to attention, and have them all blown up."

We were talking about the bad old days of amateur tennis, compared with what Rosie viewed as the glorious new regime fostered by Virginia Slims. Unlike Margaret, Rosie approved wholeheartedly of the big money. (In the first six months of 1973 she surpassed her entire 1972 Virginia Slims earnings of $40,250; by the end of the year her overall prize money totaled more than $100,000.)

"Billie Jean had won Wimbledon three or four times, and when she walked through an airport, people hardly knew her," Rosie said of amateur days. "World Champion? Who's that? You could never explain, well, I'm an amateur, but I'm really a pro, because there's no such thing as pros in our sport. You couldn't talk about money. So people thought, well, Jesus, these tennis players are just rich, rich, rich, they're from well-to-do families, it's a snobbish game. Now they know how much you're worth. They'll look at you and say, 'Oh, you're the one who made $70,000.' "

She noted that the prize money on the Slims circuit had gone from $300,000 three years ago to almost a million. "What we made in one tournament, in this tournament, you can make what a person makes in *one year*. I mean, that's incredible. Billie Jean made over $100,000 twice. Never in a million years would we have thought of making that when I started out. And the recognition—what was the attendance last night?"

It was reported at 3,422, I told her. "Well, that's pretty

good. Five years ago, that looked so impressive. Now, you look around and figure, shoot, this place should be filled; we've got the women's professional tour here!" she replied.

Rosie talked what I came to recognize as the Billie Jean King party line on subjects like these. Billie Jean took —and her clique of player-friends adopted—the general attitude that the more commercial, the more major league, the more mass media tennis became, the better off the game and its players, male and female alike, would be. Of course, they were absolutely right. Tennis was *the* game of the 1970's, and a professional sport should be run by professionals, not by the country club elite. One explanation for their militantly commercial stance was their working-class origins and the snobbery they had been subjected to as youngsters when they had played at such rich men's playgrounds as the Merion Cricket Club outside Philadelphia and Longwood in Boston. Billie Jean, the daughter of a fireman, made it perfectly clear the night she met Bobby Riggs in the commercial carnival that was the Astrodome. "Ever since I started in the sport, I wanted to change it. I thought it was just for the rich and just for the white. Ever since that day when I was eleven years old and I wasn't allowed in a photo because I wasn't wearing a tennis skirt, I knew I wanted to change the sport."

Rosie, who was nearly kicked off the courts at Wimbledon one year because her dress wasn't white, felt the same way. She rarely talked about her growing up years or her private life. But when I asked her how it had been, coexisting with the Brahmins, some of the now-submerged hurts came through.

"It was difficult," she admitted. "I was aware that other people lived differently, that other kids had money, that they could afford to go to tournaments in style, have nice cars, live in nice homes, have enough money to go out and have nice lunches." Rosie often brought her lunch in a paper bag. Sometimes she didn't bring it at all, because she couldn't afford to get to a tournament, to pay the entrance fee or to buy a pair of tennis shoes. She talked about how at junior tournaments, other kids would have the "luxury" of buying themselves "cheeseburgers, milk shakes, french fries." Rosie was describing what was, years later, still some of her favorite food . . . along with steak.

The juniors had been equally difficult for other players who came from non-Brahmin backgrounds. One night at dinner months later, Peachy, Rosie, Tory and Ceci Martinez were reminiscing about the Merion Cricket Club. "We were also so intimidated by those people—they were such snobs," Peachy recalled, adding that she finally retaliated one day by kidnapping a club mascot, a toy golden bear. They were constantly being cheated out of expense money by club officials.

Rosie sat listening quietly. Finally she said, with a snort, "Those clubs, they were somethin' else. All those rich kids. They got to play tennis all the time, and yet you'd never see a top player coming out of there, from New York or Philadelphia or Boston. The top ones, they came from Florida and California, off the public courts."

Peachy, four years older than Rosie, remembered Casals as a sullen loner on the junior circuit. "I would say hello and you would go 'Ugh.' You weren't too friendly."

Rosie shrugged, looking down at the table. "Hell, I didn't know anyone. I was a kid. I was the new girl."

Had those experiences made her a better competitor? I asked now.

"Yes," she replied, "because I wanted to *be* somebody. I knew I was good, and winning tournaments—it's kind of a way of being accepted."

Billie Jean and Rosie were accepted, grudgingly, but never welcomed by the tennis establishment. They were a little too hungry, a little too eager for public recognition, a little too ready to make tennis their careers instead of pretending to be stockbrokers who played tennis on the side. When their first chance to become pros came, in 1968, they jumped at it. Along with Francoise Durr and Ann Haydon Jones, they signed pro contracts with George Mac-Call and the four of them started out on the National Tennis

League tour with eight male pros. At last, they were legit.

Before long, the four women discovered that being a pro was no bed of roses. "There were times when we would get to a place and the court wasn't even laid down yet, when there were no tennis balls," Rosie said, noting that the Slims now traveled with a Sportface carpet laid down in each city for the group by a special crew.

Billie Jean later reminisced about the 1968 tour as being one long horror show that taught the women hard lessons about how to be professionals.

"In France, in 1968, we sometimes had to share the dressing room with the fellows. There were cobwebs, the water didn't come out of the showers, there were johns you wouldn't believe. We slept two hours a night for thirty days, traveling six hours by car and three hours by plane all in the same day. I'll never forget the time we played on asphalt that had just been poured that day. The balls got black.

"But it was a great experience for the four of us," she concluded. "We learned how to stick through it all."

It helped, both Billie Jean and Ann Jones agreed, being with men pros like Rod Laver and Pancho Gonzales who had themselves come up the hard way to pro status. "They never looked scruffy," Ann Jones said. "They never missed practice. And after a while we all had the feeling we were part of a piece somehow. It was one of the things we missed when the women's tour was formed and we were all on our own."

The growth of open tennis, and of the separate women's tour, had given Rosie and Billie Jean the status they had longed for. In addition, over the years, the two of them became close friends, doubles partners, business associates. There was only one trouble. When it came to singles play, Billie Jean "owned" Rosie. Despite Casals' denials, the record books showed that when playing King, Rosie was, in players' language, "psyched out."

"Watch them sometimes when they're playing each

other," Peachy told me. "Normally, you never look at your opponent—you look at the ball; you try to ignore the person there. But Rosie can't ignore Billie Jean. When they change sides, and they're at the umpire's chair, Rosie will sneak looks at Billie Jean. She can't shake the idea that she's playing the Old Lady."

Rosie was tired of being asked constantly why she couldn't beat King. "Look, she's Number 1 in the world!" she would say. Nevertheless, she acknowledged her Billie Jean problem. "There comes a time when you have to disassociate yourself from a friend who's your opponent. Most of the players have learned to do that. They've been competing far too long with one another to carry on the court what happened, say, if you had breakfast together. It's just two different things. You completely detach yourself. You can't think about 'Well, she's my friend . . .' or you're in trouble.

"But Billie Jean is such a difficult player to play." She sighed. "You're always tuned in to what she's doing, what she's thinking. I know her very well, so emotionally I can get involved with her, what she's thinking, instead of doing what I have to be doing."

Many players I asked about the problem of facing one's best friend across the net with thousands of dollars on the line insisted, in the words of one, "I don't see my friend, I see an opponent." Interestingly, two women who had been bothered most by the inevitability of playing friends were British—Virginia Wade and her onetime doubles partner, the now-retired Ann Jones. "I'd rather play anybody in singles than the person I'm in doubles with," Ann Jones said candidly. "It's one of the toughest assignments in tennis." Virginia said it hurt her so much when she beat Ann that they had to stop traveling together. Both felt that perhaps players could be real friends only with those far above or far below their own level of competition.

The American women seemed far less disturbed by the issue. However, Jeanne Evert, Chris's younger sister, who at fifteen was either still young enough to be honest about the problem or not old enough to steel herself against it, acknowledged conflicting emotions about playing Chris. "We practice together all the time," Jeanne said, "and suddenly one day it counts. She's my sister. I can't get that out of my mind."

For Jeanne, Chris would always be Number 1. For Rosie, Billie Jean filled that role, although by the end of 1973 Rosie had begun to turn the tide. Somehow, it was this failing—if that's the right word—that endeared both Jeanne and Rosie to me. It was part of the warmth in both of them. Rosie was perhaps the most popular player among her colleagues because they could sense the warmth beneath that tough-Indian surface of hers. It was said that she "carried" her friends in certain matches—gave them a few games—when she was confident she could beat them. "She was good to her friends," Carol Garcia, a buddy from Golden Gate Park, told interviewer Thomas Carter of Casals' earliest tennis playing days. "In tournaments she'd give them sets to make them look good." Tory Fretz, a solid but far from championship-caliber player who suffered like Job from the psychological block Billie Jean called "El Choko," was a buddy of Rosie's who, on paper, should have lost to Casals badly. But at Wimbledon, the score of their third-round match was 7-5, 7-5. A few months later, in Houston, it was 3-6, 6-0, 6-2. During the Houston match, those who knew both women exchanged knowing glances. When I suggested afterward that she had been kind in the first set, Rosie coolly dismissed the idea. "Shit, I just forget how to play from day to day, and it takes me a set to learn again."

In many ways, Rosie was the Liza Minnelli of women's tennis. Like the Minnelli characters in *The Sterile Cuckoo* and *Cabaret,* she was the unbeautiful gamin who found refuge from her insecurities by playing the part of either kook or clown. There was no player I more enjoyed watching. There was no player more conscious of the crowd. She was the most outrageous ham on the circuit. In one match against Janet Newberry, a good shot by Janet skidded deep into Rosie's forehand corner, Rosie dashed over, nearly overran the ball, and then smashed it crosscourt from *between her legs* for an outright winner that gave her the game. The crowd roared. Janet shook her head and smiled helplessly at the Academy Award performance. As Rosie sauntered to the sidelines, she shot a sly grin at friends in the front row of boxes and said, "It's the only way to hit a forehand!"

Perfume in the Locker Room

TEDDY TINLING WAS SITTING IN A FRONT ROW BOX, STARing at Kerry Harris's panties.

"That dress should be two inches longer in back," he said, as Harris, a big-boned Australian, bent over to receive Lesley Hunt's serve, revealing a vast expanse of pink ruffled underpants. "The fact is," he said to no one in particular, "she wants to show her ass."

Tinling, the official dress designer for Virginia Slims, was quite a sight himself. Sixty-two years old, 6 feet 5 inches tall, his head totally shaved, with a long oval face and enormous pointy ears, a see-through blue shirt unbuttoned to midchest, an array of hippie beads and gold chains dangling from his neck, he looked like an older, elongated version of Spaak of "Star Trek." Teddy ("Call me Ted from now on —my agent tells me Teddy sounds too Minnie Mouse") was an English couturier who had made a career of designing clothes for just about every major woman tennis player since Suzanne Lenglen. He was a nonstop talker with nonstop opinions that were as outsized as his body, a man who thirsted for recognition but who said that he had refused to design clothes for the German and Russian players because "I don't like Germans and I don't like Russians. I've been through two wars and I've seen what they're like." He also was an unquestioned authority on women's tennis. Here at the Palestra Saturday night he had pronounced the first semifinal, Hunt versus Harris, as "the worst ever." The real finals, he said, would be the second semifinal match between Court and Casals.

Tinling wasn't the only strange creature I was sitting with. Next to him was James Van Alen, an elderly gentleman with a pink face that looked like a rubber ball, who ran the Newport Casino tennis courts and the National Lawn Tennis Hall of Fame. He spoke with a pronounced English accent although he was an American, because he had gone to Cambridge and never let anyone forget it.

In Van Alen's hand was a stick with a red flag on the end of it. It seemed that in addition to being the inventor of VASSS—the Van Alen Streamlined System (instead of the 15,30,40, the points were counted 1,2,3,4, with no Advantage)—that was being used in some tournaments, he had also designed the nine-point "sudden death" tie breaker used to decide sets after the score had reached 6-all. To promote "sudden death," Van Alen had devised the flag, which umpires were supposed to hoist as a tie breaker began. When Van Alen came to a tournament, he always brought along a spare flag. He sat holding it, like a kid with a circus pennant, while keeping up a loud conversation with the five other people in the box. Midway through the match, Lesley Hunt finally turned to our corner and whispered, "Sshhh!" Harris, an improving player with a blasting first serve, took the match in three sets 6-4, 4-6, 6-2, and Van Alen's flag stayed by his side.

He got to hoist it in the first set of the next match. Rosie, in a shocking-pink dress, and Margaret, in a white one with a familiar large collar (she liked to have it snuggling around her neck), were playing as evenly as two players could. It was a classic confrontation—Rosie, the Little Engine That Could, steaming toward the net after her strong, deep serves, then suddenly throwing herself into reverse to chug back to the baseline to retrieve a lob—Margaret, a B-52 Bomber, swooping down from the service line in two big strides, crunching forehand and backhand volleys that exploded—pop! pop!—all over the court. Both were serve-and-volleyers, but while Rosie had to scramble back and forth, Margaret, with her height and reach advantage, seemed only to have to stretch to get to the ball.

The fans at the Palestra were on Rosie's side, as always. "I'm what's known as a crowd-pleaser," she once said. "I'm not a disciplined player. I don't play the shots that are there, but the shots that I *feel.*"

Margaret Court played the shots that were there. She was a disciplined person. While Margaret went home each night and had a few quiet beers, Rosie went out and had a few noisy ones. (A few nights earlier, she and Peachy had nearly been thrown out of the Penn Center Inn bar after Rosie, in Peachy's blonde wig, had plunked herself down at the piano and begun to knock out some tunes.)

Before this semifinal began, I had asked Rosie if she had a psychological block against Margaret, whom she hadn't beaten in five years. Rosie answered firmly, "I definitely think she's beatable. Whenever I walk on the court I always think I can win, or else I wouldn't bother to come. But when you get to really top players like Margaret or Billie Jean, it's a psychological thing. Technically our games are all basically the same. But psychologically, some girls are tougher than others."

At sudden death in this first set (whoever wins five points first wins the set), Rosie slammed two serves past Margaret, and amid an uproar among the fans because the umpire kept announcing the score wrong, won the tie breaker 5-1.

I was fascinated, more by the women and their mannerisms than by the strokes they displayed. Every emotion showed on Rosie's face; there was an angry determination in her eyes that was almost frightening. When she made an error she would throw a murderous glance at the ceiling; when she got a bad call, it would be directed at the linesman. A fan shouted out, "Bad call!" on one such mistake. Rosie smacked a ball into the stands at him. Margaret was less openly emotional, but when she made an error, she would squeeze her eyes shut, clench her fists at her side.

During the changeovers, beside the umpire's chair, Rosie would sprinkle water on her racquet grip to cool it off, then dry it with a towel. Margaret would sprawl on a chair staring at her husband, who sat, as always, across from the umpire's chair where his wife could easily see him.

They were mannerisms I saw in the two players time and time again, just as I saw those of others. Margaret, for instance, had a habit of carefully wiping her right hand on the side of her skirt after many points, so that by the end of a match there would be a faint stain at hip level. Virginia Wade, Britain's finest woman player, would constantly twist her racquet like a corkscrew in her hands waiting for a serve. Julie Heldman would stand at the service line and then suddenly do a low knee bend, as if going into a catcher's squat. Lesley Hunt would blow on her curled fingers, then wipe them on her tunic. Chris Evert would grunt on almost every serve, and emit a strange, chirping "Ooo" when she missed an easy shot. Tory Fretz would march around in a small circle, blowing out her cheeks, when she needed to calm herself down. Julie Anthony would put her hand underneath the knot of her waist-long ponytail and flip it up over her forehead. Billie Jean King, the queen of mannerisms, would run her fingers through her hair, do little tap steps when she was happy, throw her head back and raise fists toward the heavens when she was mad.

Some of the mannerisms were unconscious, others deliberate. But all were employed by the players to relax themselves, to spin off some of the incredible tension that built up during a match.

By the middle of the second set, Court and Casals had something else going during the changeovers besides their regular routines, however. Each would wait for the other to retake the court first. Margaret liked to change quickly, keep her rhythm. Rosie was trying to break it by hanging back. The changeovers got longer and longer, until it was like an Alphonse-Gaston routine.

The second set was as even as the first. But after Rosie saved one set point on her own serve when Margaret was ahead 6-5 with a beautifully angled overhead smash, Margaret swept the tie breaker 5-0. At two games all in the final set, Rosie double-faulted to lose her service.

When she lost another service game to make it 5-2, the changeover fun and games were over. Head bowed, Rosie walked onto the court first. Margaret took the match with an ace. But it was Rosie the fans stood and cheered, the applause following her all the way to the locker room. "That," stated Betty Stove, the towering Dutch player, "was the best match so far on the circuit." The final score was 6-7, 7-6, 6-2.

It was time for the post-match press conference. This time, however, instead of bringing the players into the interview room, Marilyn Fernberger invited the reporters into the dressing room. On first glance, it looked no different from the locker rooms you'd find in Madison Square Garden, the Orange Bowl or any other arena. Towels were strewn about, a table was piled high with rubbing oils, and two sweaty athletes were sprawled on stools.

There was a difference, though. Amid the towels were brassieres and bikini panties, and next to the rubbing oils were cans of hair spray and vials of perfume.

The reporters, all men except for me, giggled like schoolgirls as they trooped in. But their questions were strictly business. "What was the turning point, Rosie?" someone asked.

"The service break in the third set," she replied.

"Rosie was serving very deep so it was difficult to do anything with the ball," Margaret put in.

Casals took a cigarette out of the hands of a visitor (she was one of the few players who smoked). "A good athlete's got to puff," she said with a weary grin, accepting a beer from Stella Lachowicz, the Virginia Slims public relations director for the tour. Rosie peeled off a socklet, noticing a blister forming on her big toe. "Thanks, Margaret," she said, wiggling the toe in Court's direction.

After a dozen more questions, it was time for Court to go back inside for a doubles match. "Did you have a beer yet?" Marilyn Fernberger asked Margaret. (The Courts were known to be very fond of lager.) "I had a quarter of one and I figured that was enough." But she grabbed a can from Stella anyway, took one last swig and walked out.

Rosie remained on her stool, smoking. Much later, when Margaret returned to the locker room, there was a single can of beer left in the cooler. A message written on surgical tape was pasted to it. It said: "Mag! Love and kisses. Casals."

It was well after midnight by the time the last of us straggled out of the Palestra. Play was to resume at one o'clock Sunday afternoon, with a consolation "pro-set" (eight games to win instead of six) for third place between Rosie and Lesley Hunt. But when a bunch of us gathered in the lobby of the hotel for some serious Saturday night partying, Rosie was there, along with Stella, Tory, Wendy and a few sportswriters.

We wound up in a self-consciously hip, double-decker bar and discotheque appropriately called the Artemis, where everyone proceeded to get tanked. At 3 A.M., when the management finally threw us out, Rosie, still going strong, was drunkenly unbuttoning a sportswriter's shirt (she got to his belt, then stopped), Stella was murmuring sweet nothings in Polish to the bartender, a woman friend of Tory's was describing to me a tournament match she once played on an acid trip, and Wendy, who had assured everyone she had to be up early for church the next morning, was riding off into the night with a handsome acquaintance.

I got to the Palestra at one Sunday afternoon to watch the finals, my head pounding like a drum. I found Rosie already dressed in a lavender Tinling creation, showing no aftereffects. "Oh, I've been up for hours," she said. Wendy was absent, having missed a heat-treatment appointment with Al Marchfeld.

Rosie won the consolation match—barely—9-7, drap-

Billie Jean practicing

LEFT Chris Evert serving and ABOVE watching from sidelines

Kristien Kemmer making up before a match as Kathy Kuykendall watches

THE JERSEY SHORE TENNIS CLASSIC

Allaire Racquet Club
Wall Township, N.J.

SINGLES

$30,000 Prize Money
August 13-19, 1973

SEEDS

1. COURT
2. KING
3. CASALS
4. MELVILLE
5. NEWBERRY
6. ZIEGENFUSS
7. HUNT
8. STOVE

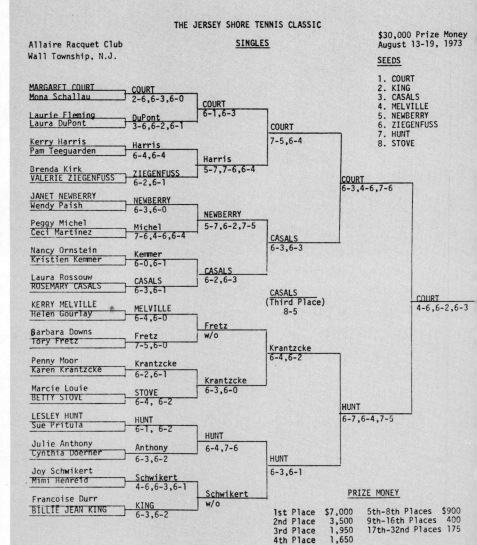

MARGARET COURT
Mona Schallau — COURT 2-6,6-3,6-0

Laurie Fleming
Laura DuPont — DuPont 3-6,6-2,6-1

COURT 6-1,6-3

Kerry Harris
Pam Teeguarden — Harris 6-4,6-4

Brenda Kirk
VALERIE ZIEGENFUSS — ZIEGENFUSS 6-2,6-1

Harris 5-7,7-6,6-4

COURT 7-5,6-4

JANET NEWBERRY
Wendy Paish — NEWBERRY 6-3,6-0

Peggy Michel
Ceci Martinez — Michel 7-6,4-6,6-4

NEWBERRY 5-7,6-2,7-5

Nancy Ornstein
Kristien Kemmer — Kemmer 6-0,6-1

Laura Rossouw
ROSEMARY CASALS — CASALS 6-3,6-1

CASALS 6-2,6-3

CASALS 6-3,6-3

COURT 6-3,4-6,7-6

KERRY MELVILLE
Helen Gourlay — MELVILLE 6-4,6-0

Barbara Downs
Tory Fretz — Fretz 7-5,6-0

Fretz w/o

Penny Moor
Karen Krantzcke — Krantzcke 6-2,6-1

Marcie Louie
BETTY STOVE — STOVE 6-4, 6-2

Krantzcke 6-3,6-0

Krantzcke 6-4,6-2

CASALS
(Third Place)
8-5

COURT 4-6,6-2,6-3

LESLEY HUNT
Sue Pritula — HUNT 6-1, 6-2

Julie Anthony
Cynthia Doerner — Anthony 6-3,6-2

HUNT 6-4,7-6

Joy Schwikert
Mimi Henreid — Schwikert 4-6,6-3,6-1

Francoise Durr
BILLIE JEAN KING — KING 6-3,6-2

Schwikert w/o

HUNT 6-3,6-1

HUNT 6-7,6-4,7-5

PRIZE MONEY

1st Place	$7,000	5th-8th Places	$900
2nd Place	3,500	9th-16th Places	400
3rd Place	1,950	17th-32nd Places	175
4th Place	1,650		

BALLBUSTERS

The 1974 Virginia Slims Tennis Circuit

You've come a long way, baby.

Virginia Slims of Washington.

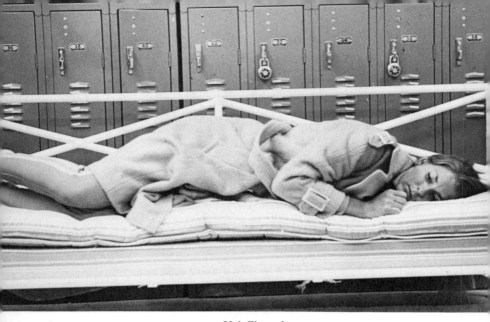

Val Ziegenfuss

Billie Jean at the inevitable post-match interview

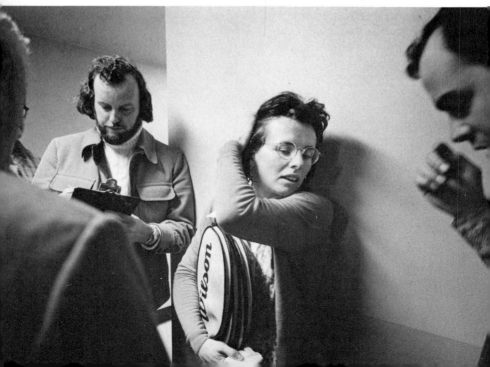

"Doc" Anthony on court
and at home in California

ing herself over the net like a wet towel at the end as Hunt came toward her to shake hands. The final between Court and Harris was a mismatch. "Some players, like Rosie, get psyched up for Margaret," Tory remarked. "Others get psyched out." Kerry Harris, a determined player from Melbourne who was in her first final on the tour after working her way up from the qualifying rounds, was never in the match. The first set sped by, 6-1.

In the Palestra office, Marilyn and Ed Fernberger glanced nervously at the clock. Princess Grace of Monaco, who started out as Grace Kelly of Philadelphia, was in town that weekend and had consented to appear at 3 P.M. to star in the winner's check-and-trophy presentation ceremony. It was now 2:30. "Come on, Kerry, dammit, get in the match!" Ed Fernberger said angrily. She didn't, and at 3 P.M., with no Princess in sight, Margaret had picked up another victory, 6-1, 6-0. The Fernbergers walked out onto the center of the court to do the honors themselves, grinning as they handed envelopes with nothing inside them to Harris and Court. (The night before, Ed Fernberger had learned to his dismay that General Foods had not yet sent him the prize money checks.)

The ceremonies finished, the two players went into the interview room for still another press conference. A reporter asked Kerry what, if she had the match to play over again, she would do differently. "Find myself another opponent," she answered, disconsolately.

The afternoon seemed like an anticlimax to me. It must have been to the fans: nearly 4,000 came Friday night to see the semifinals, but there appeared to be less than 2,500 that afternoon. Secretly, I was disappointed, too, that Princess Grace had not shown up. When I was a child, she had been my favorite movie actress, a Grace who fit her name, a woman with class, a lady. In my childhood conflict between being an athlete and being a girl, Grace Kelly, not Babe Zaharias or Maureen Connolly, was my idol. This Sunday, I was more excited by the prospect of finally

67

seeing Grace Kelly in the flesh than I was by the Max-Pax Coffee Tennis Classic.

I was sitting in the empty box that had been set aside for Princess Grace's entourage, watching the doubles final, playing with my "Ginny," a brass charm on a chain in the shape of the Virginia Slims cartoon figure. Marilyn Fernberger had given it to me; it was the first of a bunch of tennis gadgets I picked up. (That weekend I had also gotten a free pair of the Billie Jean King Adidas sneakers; a T-shirt from The Athlete's Foot, a local sporting goods store; and a Max-Pax T-shirt. By the end of the year, I had collected five more T-shirts, three grass-stained Wimbledon tennis balls, and a set of Hai Karate toiletries straight from the hand of Bobby Riggs.)

Suddenly, there was a rustle of activity behind me, and Marilyn Fernberger practically yanked me out of my seat. The Princess had arrived. I stood, gaping, as she and her family were ushered into the box. I was appalled.

Was this the movie queen Frank Sinatra fell in love with in *High Society,* this rather plain middle-aged matron with her hair all tucked up under an unattractive turban, this square-jawed, pointy-nosed woman with spectacles on? Marilyn Fernberger was urgently asking me in hushed tones if I would please give back the "Ginny," since she needed extras to give to Princess Grace's daughters. I turned it over willingly. It was the least I could do.

Idols, I decided on the Metroliner back to New York, whether athletic or otherwise, should never be allowed to grow old.

St. Petersburg

Summer Camp

THE SLIMS TOUR HAD STRUCK ME AS SOMETHING LIKE A Broadway road show company. The U.S.L.T.A. tour was more like summer camp. The St. Petersburg Masters Tennis Championship, the last stop on the eight-week spring circuit, was professional enough in its prize money—$20,000, with a $5,000 first prize—but it had an informal, camplike atmosphere about it that was a sharp contrast to the cigarette-samples-and-coffee-can commercialism of the Max-Pax.

So far, the tour had been an Evert rout, with Chris winning five of the six tournaments she had entered. She had taken a rest one week, allowing Evonne to win a tournament. The only time she was beaten was by Virginia Wade, in a three-set duel in Dallas. Moreover, St. Petersburg marked the fourth time in eight that the matches would be played on Chris's home turf—Florida clay.

The tournament was held in Bartlett Park, a public recreation area set in a middle-class neighborhood of neat lawns, small retirement homes and motels. The first things I noticed when I got there were not the seventeen Har-Tru tennis courts but the shuffleboard alleys, where dozens of old folks, oblivious to the tournament, played for nickel stakes each day. The principal tennis court was surrounded on three sides by rickety wooden stands, the kind they have around the baseball diamonds in Central Park. Di-

71

rectly behind it was a teenagers' rec hall that blared soul music so loud it looked as if the tennis players were moving to its rhythm. Nor was that the only distraction the players had to contend with. The overpowering smell of fresh bread wafted over the courts from the nearby Dandee Bakery. And the tournament directors thought nothing of announcing "The refreshment stands are now open" right in the middle of an opening-round match.

The weather was near perfect for outdoor tennis in St. Petersburg the third week in April—temperatures in the high 80's, a balmy breeze occasionally cutting through the Florida humidity.

As each player checked in at the "hospitality desk" at the start of the week, she was given an envelope with a "Welcome to the 1973 St. Petersburg Masters Tournament" letter in it, a map of tourist attractions and a list of phone numbers, and then assigned to one of the private homes where she would be spending the week. (Would the hospitality lady say, "Susan and Joan, bunk three"?) More than a dozen players were lined up to stay, gratis, at the Albermarle, a nondescript retirement hotel a few blocks away. When one of the young qualifiers found out she was booked there, she protested to the hospitality chairman.

"Can't you switch me to a home? I've only won $200 so far," she explained. At the Albermarle, she would have to buy her own meals; if she were "staying with people," she would be invited to take meals with them. She would also be able to do her laundry in their washing machine, and when you were a qualifier every dime counted.

As with the Slims, the tournament was organized first with a series of "qualifying rounds" in which the poorer players battled one another for a shot at eight places in the regular tournament draw of thirty-two. Qualifiers didn't earn a penny for playing the first qualifying round, only $50 if they lost in the second. Margaret Court might have "stayed with people" because she liked to; Nancy Spencer and Sue Mappin did it because they had to.

Nancy was a young teaching pro from Corpus Christi,

Texas, Sue a twenty-five-year-old pro from England. Monday and Tuesday of each tournament week belonged to them and the other qualifiers. The stars usually didn't arrive until Wednesday, when the first round of the "championship" draw got under way.

"Every week it's been kind of dicey whether we're going to get meals," Mappin was saying as we sat under a large tent in the refreshment area.

"Oh well, it's been good for the experience, and we'll go home with a nice suntan," said her friend, Wendy Hilliar, another Englishwoman. Sue had won $850 on the tour, Wendy $550. After paying for their airfare, meals, and gifts, they expected to break even for the two months. They had arrived in St. Petersburg after a ten-hour bus ride from Miami, interrupted at one point while the bus driver fixed a flat tire. Now, on the verge of returning home to Europe, they were complaining to Spence Conley, the tour public relations director, about not getting enough to eat.

Conley, a former newspaperman who had covered tennis and other pro sports before going into public relations, tried to pacify them. "Look," he said, "this tour was put together in two weeks and we still managed to come up with a quarter of a million in prize money. You're a professional tennis player. Someday, you're gonna play New York, the prize money will be $100,000, but you'll pay for your own transportation, your meals, your hotel. You won't have all the nice hospitality, but it'll all be worthwhile because you'll be picking up $600 a shot each round you win."

Nancy Spencer wasn't complaining about anything; she had won her first qualifying round that day, after having lost every match for seven weeks. "You just hope it's gonna get better," she said the next day as she prepared to play another qualifier who had creamed her the last time they had met.

It didn't get better. The match was on a side court, right next to which a few St. Petersburg residents were having a hit. There was no umpire, no linesman, two ball boys, and six people watching from the stands. Two of them were Nancy's grandparents, who lived in a mobile home nearby. Nancy dropped the first set 6-4, then went behind 5-2 in the second. She was good enough to teach, good enough to make a player like me feel like a quadraplegic, but she was a Double-A .220 hitter who didn't have a prayer in the majors, a tennis player who would get no closer to Wimbledon than her television set. A long lob beyond her reach, and it was all over. As she wiped her face with a towel at the deserted umpire's chair, I asked what had been going through her mind on the final point.

"That it wasn't going to be the final point," she replied matter-of-factly, and went off with her grandparents to get fed.

It wasn't just the atmosphere of Bartlett Park that reminded me of summer camp, it was the youthfulness of so many of the players and the way they interacted with the nonplaying, older tour officials as well. The U.S.L.T.A. circuit featured several players still in their teens. They were still officially amateurs and thus unable to accept prize money. They were also still in high school.

On Tuesday, at a casual press conference called to introduce local reporters to Chris Evert, Evonne Goolagong and the other name attractions, Marita Redondo, a seventeen-year-old California girl on Easter vacation from Our Lady of Peace High School in San Diego, was shyly answering a sportswriter's question about her forehand when Jeanne Evert, Chris's fifteen-year-old sister, wandered over.

"How's the homework coming?" Jeanne asked.

"Oh, like this teacher wanted to give me a 'fail' because I haven't cracked a book!" replied Marita, a slender, olive-skinned girl with a striking Oriental face. Her father was Filipino, her mother American. "I brought a book with me . . . some Russian guy . . . *Fathers and Sons.*"

Jeanne, her jaw working furiously on a piece of gum, nodded sympathetically. "Yeah, we have to read a book for religion. . . . Oh, no!" she said, suddenly remembering, "I forgot to bring it!" Later in the week, I brought up the subject of homework again as Jeanne, a vivacious, plump little girl who is both prettier and more outgoing than Chris, lay on her hotel room bed thumbing through a movie magazine. "I'm lucky," she said, "school comes easy to me, like math, I get straight A's. Who can study at a tournament, anyway?" That summer, Jeanne turned pro a month before her sixteenth birthday, while Chris missed graduation at St. Thomas Aquinas High School in Fort Lauderdale because she was busy getting to the finals at Wimbledon. (With a nice sense of the absurd, her classmates voted her "most likely to succeed.")

One sixteen-year-old did not even bother to go to high school, but was privately tutored so that she could spend more time playing tennis. She had a high school equivalency diploma, but according to one tour official, could understand math only in terms of tournament prizes. "If the total prize money is $10,000," the tour official would say, trying to teach her, "and the winner gets one third of that, how much would that be?"

The amount of time the players spent in the insular world of tennis tournaments reinforced a camper-counselor relationship between them and the "adults" on the circuit. In St. Petersburg, the adults included Spence Conley; Vic Edwards, Evonne Goolagong's coach and guardian; Colette Evert, Chris and Jeanne's mother; and Florence Blanchard, the wife of Mike Blanchard, the tour's referee. The role of the counselors was to chauffeur the players around, fuss over their clothing, make sure they ate properly, comfort them when they lost and scold them when necessary.

At the end of the week, for example, Sharon Walsh was about to be driven to the airport to meet her mother. Sharon, an emotional girl of twenty-one, had been seeded eighth (a new seeding was drawn up for each tournament depending on players' records in previous weeks). Much to her embarrassment, Sharon had been knocked out of the singles in the first round. She had played so poorly she had begun to cry on court. As she climbed into the car, she said to her hostess in the tone a naughty camper would use the day before Visiting Sunday, "Listen—don't say a *thing* to Mother about what happened this week!"

Flo Blanchard was frequently called on to play mother superior to some of the players, most especially Patti Hogan, an articulate, freckled tournament veteran with an explosive Irish temper that made Pegeen Mike of *Playboy of the Western World* seem catatonic.

In the first round on Wednesday, Patti, who was twenty-three, was struggling against a sixteen-year-old imitation-Chris Evert baseliner named Rayni Fox when Flo and I took seats directly behind her in the stands. Patti had won the first set, but now she was falling behind and periodically bouncing her Wilson steel racquet off the clay in disgust. Finally, Flo Blanchard called out, "Start moving!" Hogan turned around, gave her a hangdog look and said, near tears, "I just can't hit the ball hard enough, Flo!"

"Play like you did the other night . . . move those twinkle toes," Flo yelled. When the umpire called a shot by Fox good that Hogan insisted was out, Patti at first refused to concede the point. Then she turned to Mrs. Blanchard for reassurance. Instead, Flo said quietly, "It was in, Patti."

"Flo, I was standing right there!" Patti cried, as if she were arguing with a counselor over latrine duty. "Just play, Patti," Flo replied. Hogan won the match.

Wendy Overton had told me that an important difference between the men and the women pros was that the women were far more moody and emotional. Patti Hogan was without question top seed in that department, a player who could hit every note on the manic-depressive scale in the space of three hours. When she wanted to be, she was as good as her Number-6-in-the-United-States ranking, a player with a wily combination of what *Boston Globe* columnist Bud Collins called "crunch and junk" shots. Against Rayni Fox, she played a smart first set, throwing Fox's machinelike baseline game off with underspin backhands, blooping forehands and skittering serves interspersed with crisp, pounding overheads. But one bad call, one comment from the crowd, one dead bounce could send her into a paroxysm of rage. She would storm from one side of the net to the other, shoulders hunched over, screaming at everyone within hearing range. "This has got to be the rudest crowd I've ever seen!" she shouted at the top of her lungs when the sparse audience at the Fox match ignorantly applauded one of her errors. Some players, most notably Billie Jean, psyched themselves up or calmed themselves down when they blew up like this; Patti simply destroyed what little concentration she had. In the match with Rayni, she caught hold of herself in time. At Forest Hills, five months later, against Julie Anthony, she didn't. Patti was ahead 2-1 in the first set against Julie when she went into her tantrum. Having witnessed them before, I knew at that moment, regardless of the score, Patti was finished. She netted one ball after the next. At 1-5 in the second set the umpire said routinely, "New balls." Patti looked up and said bitterly, "Why bother?"

Patti had been warned at regular intervals throughout her career to control herself or risk suspension. Umpires fumed at her antics; after the Fox match the St. Petersburg umpire muttered, "Quite an exhibition, huh? She ought to be barred." Many players hated to face her because they regarded the tantrums as showboating, calculated moves designed to throw off her opponent's concentration.

Patti herself belittled her reputation. "Hell, if I were with the Slims, I wouldn't even rank twelfth in the racquet-throwing department." She bragged about hitting a ball so far out of one country club court it landed in the swimming pool. "Why do I have a temper? Look at my last name."

But Patti's tantrums went far beyond the realm of "Irish temperament." More than one player told me that her hysteric behavior could be blamed in part on her father who had, when she was younger, hit her if she lost.

What was most remarkable to me was that off court, Patti could be a charming, intelligent and witty person. Talking one day about the poor prize money at major championships like Wimbledon compared to the hefty $25,000

prize at the Virginia Slims Boca Raton tournament, Patti
said, "Look, you've gotta ask yourself, Do you want to be
known as Wimbledon champ, or the champ of Boca
Raton?" Reporters ate up her quotes at press conferences,
where, her bright blue eyes twinkling, she would reel off
one-liners with the assurance of a stand-up comedian. It was
as if she aimed to win back, off court, the respect and affection she lost on court daily.

In the quarterfinal round of St. Petersburg, Patti came
up against Goolagong. It was played in the evening, under
lights so poor the ball seemed to disappear from view when
it went more than a foot above the net. Patti, hardly a
speedy player, chugged after Evonne's effortless shots, first
to one alley, then to the other; when Evonne went after
Patti's shots, she seemed to skim the surface of the clay.
The wind played games of its own with the ball. Down one
set and love-30 the first game of the second, Patti, who had
been keeping fairly quiet, said—more confused than angry
—"I can't figure out which way it's blowing!" From the
stands a fan answered, "That way!" "Thank you!" she
shouted back. The final score was 6-2, 6-1. In the clubhouse
lounge that also served as interview room, a reporter asked
Evonne later whether the lights had bothered her. "She
doesn't have to see that well," Patti butted in, "she hits by
radar."

That night, Patti and I went out together for a few
drinks. Most of the women players were light drinkers who
generally stuck to beer when they were on a night out, although Kris Kemmer could put away her share of wine, and
Vicky Berner, a minor Slims player, liked to have a few
belts once in a while. So did Patti. Over gin and tonics, we
spent a few hours rehashing tennis politics along with Edy
McGoldrick, the U.S.L.T.A. official in charge of women's
affairs. At one point I complained that she had told me more
than I ever wanted to know about the subject. "But don't
you understand?" she said with a grin. "The politics are
more fun than the game!"

As I was driving her back to the house where she was

staying, we passed Al Lang Field, the New York Mets' spring training home. Earlier, I had asked her if she had always wanted to play tennis. "I wanted to be a left-fielder for the Red Sox," she had answered, a remark that made her my friend for life. Now, driving by the stadium, she explained that when she was a kid she had tried to join the local Little League, but it had voted to exclude girls.

"If they had let women in the Little League when I was a kid, I wouldn't be a reporter today," I said, gin having clouded the facts of my limited childhood baseball talents.

"I sure as hell wouldn't have become a tennis player," said Patti. "Couldn't you imagine, two out in the ninth, your team's down two runs, it's the World Series, you're up at bat and pow! A home run!"

The U.S.L.T.A. tour was dubbed the "Ev and Chrissie Show" by sportswriters because its stars, Evonne Goolagong and Chris Evert, dominated most of the tournaments and got the lion's share of attention from the press. In the early weeks, it had as added attractions Virginia Wade of Britain and Olga Morozova, the best woman player from the Soviet Union, but both had dropped out halfway through the spring season. Besides Hogan, Walsh, Redondo and Jeanne Evert, the remainder of the players were almost all foreigners, a few of whom were on their first visit to the United States.

The most promising newcomer among the foreigners was Martina Navratilova, a large, square sixteen-year-old Czech left-hander whose high Slavic cheekbones and boyish manner suggested she would look just as at home in a Prague shoe factory as on a tennis court. One afternoon she was sitting around the Bartlett Park lounge, munching a hamburger, when Patti Hogan started kidding her about being the "pancake champ" of the tour.

Martina giggled. "I cahn't beeleef I ate da whole t'ing," she said, pointing to her T-shirt, which was emblazoned with the same motto.

Martina's first American trip had been an orgy of junk

79

food; the lures of capitalist pancake and burger franchises had proved so enticing that she had gained ten pounds in eight weeks. "I hof to borrow all new clothes," she explained, "even my feet get bigger!"

Food, growth and dieting were a constant subject of discussion among players. Players like Hogan, Billie Jean King, Jeanne Evert and Janet Newberry, who tended toward being overweight, were constantly on diets. Billie Jean, who in her early years had been a chunky 142-pounder, had dropped 25 pounds after her first knee operation in 1968. (In the process, she had lost all the muscle tone in her legs and it took her a year to regain her championship form.) She had gradually gained most of the weight back, but it was mostly in her legs, making her appear much slimmer. For the first half of the year, King was on a modified Atkins low-carbohydrate diet that one friend believed contributed to her bout with illness just before the Riggs match. After winning Wimbledon, she announced gleefully that the thing she was looking forward to most as a reward for her win was vanilla ice cream. Patti Hogan, who had a history of blowing up like a balloon, lost fifteen pounds during the year as her romance with Lance Tingay, a married British sportswriter nearly old enough to be her grandfather, blossomed.

In general, the better players ate pretty sensibly— steaks, salads, milk, eggs. They usually had big breakfasts because later meals had to be timed to fit in with their playing schedules. The rule was that players ate very lightly before a match, saving their big meal of the day for afterwards. A match late in the day meant not having dinner until ten or eleven o'clock at night. Those who stayed in hotels made much use of room service; not many of the players were adventurous eaters and it was frequently easier to order a chef's salad from the hotel kitchen, as Chris Evert liked to do, than go out and find a restaurant. Indeed, Kristien Kemmer, a sophisticated twenty-one-year-old player on the Slims circuit, was the only one I met with an inclination toward gourmet food although she was a semi-vegetarian.

More typical was Rosie Casals who, finding herself one night at a seafood restaurant, dined reluctantly on scallops, remarking that she never ate lobster because "It takes too long." Chris Evert and Billie Jean were McDonald's freaks.

Everybody had her own favorite drinks, too. Billie Jean guzzled diet Dr Pepper, Margaret Court went through two big bottles of Gatorade during a match on a hot day, and everyone drank the Cokes and orange juice provided in courtside coolers. Chris Evert occasionally took a Coke after a match, but when I visited her at home in Fort Lauderdale, I discovered that no soft drinks were allowed in the Evert family refrigerator.

As athletes, they were very conscious of their height and weight. Once asked what her immediate goal was, Jeanne Evert, barely 5 feet tall, replied, "To grow."

Julie Anthony's immediate goal was to stay skinny.

"Don't you ever wish you were bigger?" I asked.

"What do you mean?" she said indignantly. "I *am* big." She was 5 feet 6 inches and weighed all of 115 pounds. She had taken off some weight on purpose before going on the summer tour. "I got the idea from Pancho Gonzales, whose philosophy is to be as thin as you possibly can. You're carrying around less weight so you don't get as tired, and you're faster."

Lots of players joked about how they had cheated on their vital statistics in the tournament programs and record books. Leafing through the Slims program one day in New Jersey, Madeline Pegel, a cheery, chubby Swedish woman, chuckled when she read her height and weight as 5 feet 6 and 135 pounds. "Maybe I was 135 pounds a few days after I was born!"

Ceci Martinez, another Slims player, laughed along with her. "It wasn't only the weight, Peg," she said. "I looked at the magazine, saw you down there as the same age I am, and I knew *somebody* was kidding. I mean, how come I get older and everybody else stays the same age?" Madeline said nothing and smiled.

Without question, the most impressive physical development of any player took place in Chris Evert as she rose to stardom between the ages of sixteen and eighteen. The petite 5-foot-2½-inch girl with the weak serve and Barbie-doll figure who caused a sensation at Forest Hills in the 1971 U. S. Open was now a 5-foot-6-inch young woman with hefty curves and a cleavage accentuated by a tennis wardrobe made up almost entirely of scoop-necked dresses. Chris knew she looked good on the court, and she knew her extra height and poundage had put more punch in her game, but, like Marita Redondo, who was 5 feet 5 inches, 115 pounds and perfect, yet who wanted to weigh 104, Chris would have preferred to shave a few pounds.

Thus, at her first press conference in Bartlett Park after she won her first-round match on Wednesday night, she admitted that in two years she had gained ten pounds. A local sportswriter, sitting next to her on one of the lounge couches, wanted to know her current weight.

"I weigh"—she paused, squeezing her eyes as if debating whether to come out with the truth—"uh, 120." Then she reached over, put her hand on the sportswriter's knee, looked deep into his eyes and added, "But I *really* would like to be 118. Can't you just say 118?"

The Ice Dolly

CHRIS AND JEANNE EVERT WERE STAYING WITH THEIR mother, Colette, in a pair of rooms at the local Hilton. For much of the year Colette chaperoned both daughters. Goolagong and her party were also staying at the Hilton; the accommodations had been provided free. In previous years, Colette told me, the Everts had stayed at the Albermarle, but Chris had decided to accept the Hilton hospitality this time because one of the elderly Albermarle regulars had a habit of playing the piano early in the morning. More importantly, the Hilton had color television and room service, facilities the young star was getting accustomed to enjoying.

"Tennis isn't like a job to me yet and I hope it never will be," Chris, who had turned pro right after her eighteenth birthday four months before, had said Thursday morning as she and Jeanne were on their way to a practice session. I had come to Florida expecting to dislike her, precisely because from watching her play and reading the growing newspaper and magazine literature about her, she seemed to treat the game very much like a job. I thought of her as the Mark Spitz of tennis, an ambitious, cool cutey who was parlaying a carefully groomed athletic talent into a commercial conglomerate of endorsements and personal appearances, a teenaged hustler whom the media had hopped on not because her skills were that superior but

83

because her wholesome looks satisfied the sport's perpetual need for a new ingenue. Seeing her play several times in the past few years, I had been put off by what looked to be a dull, machinelike baseline game with no joy in it. Indeed, her emotionless presence on court had led the British press to label her "the Ice Dolly," the name of an ice cream pop sold at Wimbledon; some players called her "little Miss Grunt" because of the noise she made, involuntarily, each time she hit a ball with extra power.

She was not terribly popular among the other players, either the U.S.L.T.A. group or the Slims. Why should she have been? The others had slaved away in the backwaters of tennis for years, searching for their names in the agate box scores of newspaper columns, watching their skin grow coarse and their noses peel and their feet become callused as they fought for a glimmer of the limelight. Chris had seemingly billowed out of the Florida clay onto the glossy covers of national magazines full grown like a Botticelli Venus, poised, pretty, famous and rich. Men thought her adorable, little girls worshiped her, middle-aged mothers came up to her at tournaments and told her she had restored their faith in youth. She was Miss American Pie, 1973. So far this year, she had won seventeen straight matches. While Wendy Hilliar and others were scratching out $550, Chris had already earned over $36,000 by April. Not only did she almost never lose, she never seemed to sweat. (Julie Heldman told the story of a particularly tense moment in the Wightman Cup matches in 1971 when Chris, then sixteen, said, "I notice more sweat than usual on my hands—I must be reacting to the atmosphere.") No wonder her colleagues weren't crazy about her.

But Chris fooled me. She lived up to her advance billing as a cool customer, yet she was also intelligent, amusing when she was relaxed and among friends, emotional when no one was looking, relatively unspoiled, acutely aware of the pitfalls of stardom, friendly in her own reserved way and superbly graceful under pressure. On her own terms, she was a perfect young lady, so perfect I ended up liking her.

We were driving to a nearby country club for what was the first of two practice sessions that day. The players practiced every day during tournaments, most of them for an hour at some point before a match, some of them longer. The basic format was first, straight ground strokes, which the players each aimed to get in deep between the service line and the baseline, then crosscourt ground strokes angled toward the corners, then a series of lobs and overheads, then "points"—one player serving, the other receiving and playing out the rally until a ball went out. Some players went even further—Billie Jean, for example, liked to get in shape by playing two on one in practice. At Wimbledon she shouted out imaginary scores to Betty Stove and Vicky Berner, her practice partners, to get the concentration for match play: "Okay, second serve, love-30." As she played out the imaginary game, she kept up a running commentary. ". . . bad bounce, brings it up to deuce, King picks up the ball. . . ."

Practice could be as much fun to watch as real match play, since the women were looser and more verbal than they would dare to be before a crowd. At the Lakewood Country Club, where the U.S.L.T.A. players worked out, the courts sounded like a baseball stadium during a pepper game: "Come on, sock it to me . . . atta girl . . . damn, what a shot . . . harder!"

The Evert sisters were both dressed in track suits, Jeanne's all white, Chris's powder blue. As they hit to each other during the hour-long warm-up, they looked like mirror images, whirling away on their two-fisted backhands like the hockey players in pinball machine games. Chris, a model of discipline, came to the net to work on overheads, her weakest shot, shrieking like a banshee each time she missed one.

Back at the hotel, Jeanne plopped herself on the bed to read about Cher in a movie magazine while Chris showered, ate and talked. I was especially curious about her feelings on femininity on the court, since she was now its leading exponent. "No point is worth falling down over," she had told Peter Range, a *Time* magazine correspondent, that week; it epitomized the Chris Evert school of tennis.

"That's the one thing women's tennis has, is femininity," she said, plucking her eyebrows over a small hand mirror as she spoke. "If women looked like men or played like men it would be boring. I know some women who lift weights—they say Margaret Court did. But even if it would make me stronger I'd never do it. It's *important* to look feminine—for your self-confidence. I want to be known as a woman, not just as a tennis player." She kicked off her shoes, pointing to purple marks on each of her heels and the calluses on the bottom of her feet. "See, I'm already getting these. That's why after a match I like to come home and take a long hot bath."

The room was a mess, the bureau top piled high with a zillion varieties of eye shadow, mascara, lipstick, nail polish and powder. Chris never went out for a match without putting on full makeup, earrings, a pretty ribbon on her ponytail or single braid. She washed her hair with Johnson's baby shampoo every day. When, at the end of a match, an opponent often looked as though she had combed her hair with an eggbeater, Chris looked as if she had just left Elizabeth Arden's.

There were distinct differences about the issue of court appearance among players, however. Wendy Overton belonged to the Evert faction: "I think it's important as an athlete to maintain an air of femininity," she had said. "We should look nice out there. We're entertainers, people are watching our actions. You just don't show up in a pair of dirty old shorts and T-shirt anymore."

Rosie Casals didn't disagree, she just didn't think the issue was a major one. "I think my clothes look feminine enough, but I go on the court to play, and whether people like it or not, I really couldn't care less. It's very hard with women in sports, you know. Men spectators can't understand what the hell women are doing, smashing balls, killing themselves all over the court. Well, I look at it as a skill. If I were a singer, well, sure I wouldn't have muscles that show, but I'd have worked on that skill. You know," Rosie added, "the thing is, people see us in our worst moments. Photographers take pictures of us after being on the court for an hour and a half, full of perspiration. I mean, singers and dancers, they have a disguise, you don't see them unless they have all their makeup on. So the pictures of us come out, all sweaty, and people say, 'Geez, will you look at that? I wouldn't be out there for all the world looking like that.' Then, when we *do* get dressed up, when we put on our street clothes, they don't even recognize us."

Rosie, jock first, woman second. She made a face when I repeated Chris's "falling down" remark. "If a point calls for killing yourself, well, sometimes one point will turn the whole match around. You make this fantastic shot, you fall flat on your face, and that can be the psychological edge you need. It can just shatter your opponent. Suddenly pow! That's it!" She, like some others, belittled Chris's concern about looks. "If that's the image she wants, the cute little bubble-gum chewing kid from Florida, fine. That's not me."

Chris, teenage girl first, jock second. Her long honey-brown hair sometimes flew in her face; she simply braided it or twisted it up in a neat bun for a match. Billie Jean had had long hair as a young girl. It would blow in her face during matches; she cut it off.

I asked Chris if she thought the Court-Riggs match scheduled for the following month might set a trend.

"Men playing women? I hope it never comes," she said, munching on a turkey sandwich and some grapefruit slices. "Everyone knows the Number 1 woman can't beat the Number 30 man. That would be the battle of the sexes and everybody would become masculine."

I asked, out of curiosity, what she thought of Spitz. "Oh, he'll never do that well again, so it's wise for him to get into TV and movies," she said knowledgeably. But as far as her own commercial commitments went, she said, she was proceeding cautiously—a $50,000 a year contract with Puritan for endorsing a line of tennis dresses, a contract with Wilson for racquets. Not bad for an eighteen-year-old kid still in high school. Yet, she said professionally, perhaps too professionally, "The endorsements haven't changed my attitude, I mean, I still play to win. But there's more responsibility now. If I play well, my dresses will sell well."

Caution, responsibility, reserve—Chris's attitudes were as disciplined as her steady baseline game. Her personality and her style of play were all of a piece, built into her from childhood by her father. Jimmy Evert was a Fort Lauderdale teaching pro who, despite his daughter's fame, continued to give lessons for $6 a half hour at the Holiday Park public courts six blocks from the Everts' modest bungalow. He was known as a cautious, God-fearing Catholic, a man who believed in the old-fashioned virtues of savings accounts and hard work. Deeply suspicious of the quick-buck promoters, he had turned down dozens of additional commercial offers made to Chris. Chris was very much her father's daughter. They even looked alike—the same pigeon-toed walk, the small eyes too close together. After every match, Chris called her father with a complete blow-by-blow account, like a good student who brought home reports on school each day.

It had been Jimmy's idea, not Chris's, to take up tennis in the first place. Each time I asked a player if she remembered the first time she had picked up a racquet, she would respond with an immediate recollection of that moment, even if she had been only four years old at the time. When I asked Chris the same question, she replied, "No, I was too young. I was maybe six.

"I had no feeling for the game," she added calmly. "I just did it because my dad brought me over to the courts. It was his idea. I didn't *dislike* it, I mean, it was something to do. When you're eight or nine you don't really have many hobbies."

Linda Tuero, a U.S.L.T.A. player who was not in St. Petersburg, later related a similar experience, but she was less sanguine about it. A native of Metairie, Louisiana, the daughter of a Delta Airlines pilot, she was taken out on the court every day by her father at the age of ten because "my parents wanted me to do something in sports and I hadn't liked swimming."

She was hardly crazy about the idea. "What kid in the fourth grade wants to give up parties and things for working on a tennis court? If I had had my way I would have played twice a week. I got to like winning—I was Number 1 in the South by the time I was twelve. But I remember telling people, 'Oh, can't go to the party, because I had a tennis lesson, and then hoping it would rain that day. I spent so much time at tennis I had very few friends. Besides, my parents told me if I didn't make the honor roll in school, too, I wouldn't be allowed out." When I asked if she had resented her parents' pushing, however, she replied airily, "Oh, no. I can't thank them enough for what they did. It was good discipline."

Chris Evert insisted her tennis education hadn't been as cut and dried as it might sound. She grew to like hanging out at Holiday Park; she made friends and started bringing her lunch with her. Day after day, four hours at a time, she would labor to groove her now-famous baseline strokes. She never considered herself a natural athlete, although her father said she was the quickest learner among the five Evert children, of whom Chris was the next-to-eldest. (Her brother Drew, a year older, played for the Auburn team but dropped out of serious competitive tennis early. "He didn't like the pressure," Colette Evert said.) Like Margaret Court, whom she admired, Chris played the shots that were there. She hated the phrase "ball machine" because she knew it was not a compliment, resented the idea that people might prefer to watch "flashy" players. "I know I'm not a natural, but I don't think I'm a mechanic either. I've worked hard at it!" she said.

But there was another side of Chris Evert, the side she showed when she would neck with her boyfriend, Jimmy Connors, right in the middle of a court after they had practiced together, the side that longed for the parties and the fun normal teenagers were supposed to have.

Later in the year, she made the obvious decision to skip college and devote full time to tennis. In September she sat in the family room in Fort Lauderdale during a rest week, talking about returning home the week earlier and realizing that all her friends were away at college.

"I felt kinda weird," she said. "I had been going to school, you know, for twelve years, and all of a sudden I had so much time! I missed it. You associate things with school. Like the weather was getting a little bit cool, and I thought, 'Right now I'd be in school, with a little sweater on, studying.' " She looked out the window almost wistfully, and then explained, in a voice of total control, how college would have been "a real waste of time," how she had hardly touched her staggering sum of prize money because it was "security for the future." Then she left the house—to practice.

It was time for Chris to go to Bartlett Park to play her second-round match. (Jeanne, who was in the lower half of the draw, was scheduled to meet Evonne Goolagong in the featured evening match.) Jeanne braided Chris's hair and then sat herself in front of the television as we walked out.

The match was over in less than an hour, with Chris carving up Ann Kiyomura, a promising, chunky young Californian who, with her long black pigtails and dark, round Oriental face, looked like an Eskimo in a Flaherty movie. Later at the press conference, Chris noted that she liked to drop-shot a lot against "slower players, like"— she giggled—"my sister." To a reporter who asked whether she thought she might have to meet Jeanne later in the draw, Chris answered simply, "No way," predicting Jeanne would get "three games a set—no more" off Evonne.

It seemed kind of cold-blooded, but I learned that players were quite clinical about their friends' chances in upcoming matches. It was not unusual for someone to impersonally write off her buddy's—or sister's—chances against a superior opponent, only to sit in the stands two minutes later rooting mightily for her regardless of the odds.

Back at the hotel, Chris took her second shower of the day and changed into practice clothes to warm up Jeanne, who had spent the afternoon in front of the television. "I feel sorry for Jeannie," said Chris. "It's not easy, having to sit around all day waiting for a match."

We returned to Bartlett Park, where Chris gave Jeannie a combination warm-up, pep talk and strategy session for Goolagong. "What do I do if she comes to the net?" asked Jeanne, in between strokes. "Lob?"

"Yeah, to her backhand." They both cracked up on one of Chris's mis-hits. "Practice your dropshot," commanded Chris.

"I can't when I'm laughing," said Jeanne, giggling.

Chris ordered Jeanne to practice her serve as they played some points. "Don't have any mercy on me," insisted Chris, but each time she tried to come to the net on Jeanne's serve, Jeanne passed her. Chris wound up yelling, "Forget it!" By the end of the hour, they were making raucous fun of each other's misses, taking turns flinging their racquets at the net and having a wonderful, very un-Evert high time.

Colette Evert had told me that she hated to see her daughters play each other in a tournament because they were such good friends, and I could understand her feelings. They were more than sisters, they were alter egos. Jeannie, bright as a button, with her own distinct bubbly charm and bunny-teeth good looks, made being Chris Evert's younger sister look easy. "She's stronger and faster than me still," Jeanne would tell anyone who asked, "but I've got time yet." I couldn't imagine how Jeanne could maintain such equanimity in the face of an older sister like Chris, until Chris herself explained it to me.

I had asked her whether she thought Jeanne was jealous of her success, whether playing on the same circuit had stretched their friendship.

"No, it's brought us closer together," Chris said. "She has nothing to be jealous about, really, because she's always been better in almost everything than I have. She's so smart, she gets straight A's without lifting a finger. She reads books, like *The Source,* that I think are extraordinary for a fifteen-year-old girl. She's always been more outgoing than I have, and people seem to like her more. She's more warm, you know?"

Jeanne lost to Evonne that night, and Chris suffered for her. "I'm glad I'm not sitting next to Mom," she remarked as Jeanne went behind 5-0 in the first set. "Come *on,* Jeannie, just one game!" pleaded Chris to herself. Jeanne managed to get three in the second set, but her face was a mask of gloom when it was over.

To cheer her up, Peter Range and I took the Evert sisters and a girlfriend out to a nearby waterside nightclub. Peter and I felt like counselors, worrying about the girls getting "carded"—checked for proof of age. But our waitress was understanding and we celebrated nothing in particular with a bottle of champagne. After two glasses Chris was giggly-high and passing around a newspaper photo of Jimmy Connors playing golf. Jeanne told dirty jokes, flirted charmingly with Peter, and then fell asleep in her chair, cradling the empty champagne bottle, which she took back to the hotel as a souvenir.

The Jock

"EVONNE PLAYS TENNIS THE WAY BLACK PEOPLE DANCE," Chris Evert had said of Goolagong. Some would say the comment was racist, but Chris had meant it as a compliment. At twenty-two, Evonne was the most graceful player to reach the top ranks since Maria Bueno a decade before. The daughter of a half-aborigine sheep shearer, she had captured the hearts of the tennis world in 1971 by winning Wimbledon with a smile on her face, and two years later she was still charming crowds everywhere she went, even here in St. Petersburg, which one writer called "Chrissie country."

The tournament was moving toward a final clash between Evert and Goolagong, with both players sweeping through their halves of the draw in straight sets. After three weeks in the Florida sun, Evonne was toasted to a muffin brown. Her short, curly dark hair had been frosted blonde. There were light patches on her cheeks where she had peeled. Following one match, someone had asked her if the 80-plus heat had bothered her. "Nah, I like a good perspire," she answered.

The remark summed up Evonne as perfectly as "no point is worth falling down over" summed up Chris. One male pro said about Goolagong, "She's the only one of the girls who wears a jock." He was not casting aspersions on her femininity, but merely referring to the sheer ath-

leticism of her game and the sheer pleasure she showed
hitting a tennis ball. "She doesn't seem conscious of her
body at all," Julie Heldman noted, "it just works for her."

She might not have been conscious of it, but male
jocks and spectators were. If a poll were taken among other
men tennis players, Evonne would have been voted the
sexiest woman in the game. "A panther," Julie Anthony
called her, with lovely, sinewy muscles in her brown legs
that were so much more aesthetic than the thick ones in
Billie Jean's or Rosie's.

What made her most attractive on court, though, was
her demeanor. She never scowled, never argued, hardly ever
showed a tinge of regret over a mis-hit. Evonne splashed
around a tennis court with the giddy delight of a child in
a backyard kiddy pool, chuckling when she hit a winner,
chuckling when she made an error. She reminded me
of Willie Mays when he first hit the big leagues, the happy,
not-so-bright jock who loved baseball so much he played
stickball in the streets of Harlem after he had finished a
game at the Polo Grounds.

Nobody in the tennis world credited Evonne with an
excessive I.Q., but she didn't need one. She had Vic Edwards
to do her thinking for her. Edwards was a sixty-three-year-
old Australian who ran a huge tennis school in Sydney and
who had had earlier successes with Fred Stolle and Bob
Hewitt. When Evonne was nine, an associate of Edwards
had discovered her hitting balls on a rutted court, over-
grown with weeds and overrun with chickens, in the tiny
bush town of Barellan. Edwards took one look, in-
structed the head of the local tennis club to have her play
for a year with the best players in the area, brought her to
Sydney for intensive work during the next summer vacation, and eventually moved her into his home to join his
five daughters, so he could work with her year-round. He
became her legal guardian, plotting her career, shielding
her from the press, investing her earnings. (At one point
he tried, unsuccessfully, to get fees from papers that wanted
interviews with her.)

Edwards did not like the way the press asked Evonne embarrassing questions, especially about her aboriginal background. (She did not regard herself as either black or white, but as a tennis player, although in the United States she had a devoted following among black fans.) When I asked Edwards, in St. Petersburg, if I could trail after Evonne, he nearly refused me any kind of interview, and only with the intervention of Spence Conley, the tour's PR man, was I able to accompany her to practice. Edwards later told me it was Evonne who disliked meeting the press; Evonne said she did what Edwards told her to. It was a convenient arrangement for both.

"Ever watch 'Soul Train'?" she asked, fiddling with the dials on the car radio, as we drove Friday morning to Lakewood for a practice session before her semifinal match with Redondo. "Isn't it great? I love the telly here."

Evonne was the biggest pop music fan on either tour. She knew the words to every Top-Forty hit on the air, was forever stopping off at record stores to pick up Temptations and Bill Withers tapes for her portable cassette player, and kept a radio pressed to her ear in the locker room while dressing for a match. King, Casals, the Everts and nearly everyone else liked rock music, too. Rosie had a habit of hooking up a portable radio to a loudspeaker at some courts so she could practice to music; Billie Jean got herself in the mood for Bobby Riggs by singing along with "Jesus Christ Superstar" the morning of the Astrodome match.

But Evonne was definitely the champion rock fan. Vic Edwards confessed that the loud music playing constantly used to drive him mad, until one day he was headed for a match in a car with Evonne and realized she had not turned on the radio. She lost, and the next time, he made sure *he* turned on the radio as loud as it would go.

Evonne and her doubles partner and traveling companion, Janet Young, noticed a golf cart on the Lakewood grounds and joked about taking one—they called it a "Freddie Flintstone car"—back to Australia. They had tooled around in one a few weeks before while visiting

95

with Arnold Palmer at a golf club. Even though this was her first extended visit to the States, she had skipped the usual sightseeing trips when she had time off. "Sightseeing's more tiring than playing," she said with a yawn. "So is shopping. It's a dull life, really; when we're playing matches, I just like to have a nice quiet meal, watch the telly, listen to music." She had, however, gone to her first baseball game earlier in the week at Al Lang Field. "I like to see any other sport being played," she explained. She had also liked one of the Mets farm-team coaches, a handsome young man who squired her around a few nights later and took her out to shows when she came to Forest Hills late in the summer.

Her partner, Janet, a mature twenty-one-year-old with an economics degree from the University of Melbourne who clipped newspaper articles about Watergate, was one of only a handful of women on the circuit whose range of interests was broader than the dimensions of a tennis court. When they had time to relax, the majority concentrated on simple, sporty activities—Lesley Hunt went surfing, Margaret Court went fishing, Billie Jean took up golf and watched football games on TV. Sightseeing was not high on the priority list, primarily, as Evonne indicated, because it took too much out of the players. Peggy Michel, a college graduate who had joined the Slims circuit after getting a degree in child psychology from Arizona State, summed up the difficulty in a story about playing a tournament in Nashville. "We saw the Belle Meade mansion and went to the Grand Old Opry. But if you're concentrating on your game, well . . . I was going to go out to see the Hermitage too, but Val Ziegenfuss and I had to play doubles that afternoon. She warned me that it would wear me out. First I thought, 'Well, yes, but I want to see it.' Then I had to think twice and say 'I'm playing with a partner, it's a two-way thing.' I went shopping for a little while instead." It was worth it: she and Val beat Court and Hunt, the third seeds, in straight sets.

Evonne and Janet did not have to face such a choice;

they were content to take it easy. They even seemed to take it easy during practice, hitting rather desultorily for half an hour. ("Evonne's lazy," Chris Evert had said with distinct envy. "She doesn't even warm up more than a half hour.") "Some girls can hit for hours," Evonne said afterwards, "but I'd rather just have a short hit to get the feel of it, before I play."

We sat under an umbrella at one of the stone tables in between the courts, the spray from a sprinkler drifting over our shoulders every once in a while in the breeze. Were there days, I asked, when they would rather lie by a pool somewhere than go out on a hot court and play?

"Yeah, you get days like that. It's the same as people going to work. We're doing the same thing over and over again. I mean, I enjoy tennis a lot, but some days you say, 'I wish I was going sailing.'" Evonne squinted into the hot Florida sun and smiled dreamily. "Yeah, particularly on hot days, so great for sailing."

Just as concentration was Chris's strong suit, it was Evonne's weakness. Her dreaminess was the subject of intense debate on the tennis circuit. She had become famous for what she called her "walkabouts"—lapses of concentration during a match, in which she would start missing easy points, double-faulting, even forgetting the score. She was asked about it so often that one day when the issue came up, she smiled and said with a shrug, "Well, you know me, boys."

The players regarded concentration as a tennis trait more important than strokes—the ability to bear down at crucial moments, to block out everything but the little fuzz-covered ball coming at them. When they talked about tennis being a game of mental discipline, of psychology, they were talking about concentration. Julie Heldman considered Evonne a "freak" because she did not have the "arrogance, the bitchiness, the killer instinct" that Heldman believed was the quality inherent in every championship-caliber player. "Evonne's the exception—she has so much damned talent it just explodes right out of her," Heldman said. It was a talent that sometimes worked against her, since Evonne, like Casals, would play the tough shot—the cross-court backhand that just caught the chalk, the dropshot from deep at the baseline when she was not really in good position—when an easier one would do. She, too, was a crowd-pleaser. Julie Anthony, who with Heldman was the most articulate tennis critic among the women, expressed the feelings of many when she said, "I don't think that Evonne can ever attain the stature of greatness of a Billie Jean or Margaret until she gets a little bit more serious at discipline. But," she added, "maybe, like a wild animal, if you tried to discipline her it would destroy the essence that's so great about her."

Killer instinct was what every player secretly wanted but few possessed. When players talked about Billie Jean, they did not talk about her backhand or her volley, but about the way she intimidated them on the court. "You know when you stand across the net from her that there is not just a great athlete, a good thinker, but a killer," Anthony declared. And yet, undoubtedly because they were women, they voiced fears about what that instinct might do to them. "You look at the top ten or fifteen players in the world, and they have all got a pretty hard streak running down them," Heldman said.

Evonne did not, which was why crowds found her so enjoyable. Interestingly, neither Billie Jean nor Vic Edwards, nor Evonne herself, felt the lack of concentration, of the killer instinct, was her problem. Her problem was immaturity. "Evonne cares," Billie Jean remarked one day at Wimbledon. "Don't let her fool you. You can see it in her eyes, you can see it in her face. And that concentration stuff is only a big deal among the sportswriters. We all lose our concentration, but for Evonne it's an excuse. They don't let *us* use it. No," she said, "Evonne's afraid to commit herself. She's afraid to stop pleasing the crowd and start pleasing herself instead. Until she does, she's not gonna be a real champ."

"Evonne's game has improved, matured," Vic Edwards, who kept predicting Goolagong would reach her peak by 1974, said. "But her mind hasn't matured. When it does, she could be on top for years . . . except that I reckon one of these days she'll meet some handsome guy, run off and get married." When I pointed out that Court had done that, had a child, and then gone on to even greater achievements in tennis, he laughed. "Evonne couldn't manage both. She'd probably throw up her hands and say, 'The hell with it!' "

Evonne refused to speculate on marriage, future plans, or anything else beyond the next two hours. Her motto seemed to be, if it feels good, do it. "Losing doesn't really kill me," she said sweetly, in the pleasant, lilting Australian voice that Edwards had developed with elocution lessons. "If I felt I didn't play my best, well, you can't do anything about it once you get off the court. You can't play it over again." ("Losses," Rosie Casals once said, darkly, "stay with you forever.")

"Like, most of my life I suppose I'll be playing tennis," continued Evonne under the umbrella. "So I might as well enjoy it. I've won the tournaments I've always wanted to win, like Wimbledon, and if I won it again it would be great, you know? But to me, it just all depends on how I feel."

And the killer instinct? "Uh, you know," she said with an amused giggle, "I won Wimbledon without the killer instinct."

Bye Bye, Miss American Pie

"WATCH MASTHOFF WHEN THERE ARE NO LINESMEN, AND you'll see her call a dozen 'in' balls out," a player said as Helga Masthoff played Martina Navratilova in the baking heat Friday afternoon. She also had a habit, if there *were* linesmen, of positioning herself between them and the ball so they had trouble seeing shots close to the line.

Masthoff was part of the German contingent on the U.S.L.T.A. tour, a 6-foot blonde with skinny legs who always tucked her pinned-up hair under a white peaked hat that looked like an outsized jockey cap. She was quite attractive in a bland, *Vogue*-ish sort of way; Herbert Warren Wind of *The New Yorker* described her accurately as "storklike." At thirty-one, she was a veteran of international tournaments, a clever retriever who worked her shots until her opponent made a mistake.

She was also, many players claimed, a player who always gave herself the benefit of the doubt on close shots.

Several other players—Patti Hogan and Pam Teeguarden among them—had such reputations. The practice was frowned upon, but it was also accepted as a fact of life in the big leagues. "Everybody takes points," Julie Heldman said. "Five, six years ago I believed in giving and taking 'em back, and I got screwed five matches in a row." Rosie Casals viewed the matter philosophically. "Let's say some players will give you the benefit of the doubt and others won't. Like Margaret, she may know a ball is in, in her mind and in her heart. But there's no way she'll give you the benefit of the doubt." Julie Anthony, on the other hand, was appalled when, watching Janet Newberry play Francoise Durr, Francoise kept silent after the umpire called out a wrong score in Durr's favor, giving her the game. "Frankie was walking right off the court when Janet woke up and said, 'Hey, no, it's deuce.' The ump called the correct score and Frankie turned right around and walked back on. She *knew* it. That was just more cutthroat than I had imagined," Anthony said.

Whether Masthoff had used any of her alleged tricks against Navratilova, I couldn't tell. But if she had, they hadn't done much good. Gradually wilting in the heat like edelweiss in a hothouse, she dropped the match and stumbled blindly toward the locker room, mumbling in heavily accented English, "Oh, I'm zzzoo exhausted!"

I wanted to chat; she wanted to skip town. We struck a bargain—I would drive her first to the Albermarle to pick up her gear and then to the airport. Her flight, she informed me, left at 5 P.M. It was then nearly four, and the Tampa airport was forty-five minutes away. She took a quick shower and then went in search of the tournament referee, who borrowed $420 in cash from the gate receipts to pay her. (As a quarterfinal loser, she had actually won $600, but 30 percent of that was deducted for American taxes as it was from the checks of all foreign players.)

As he was counting out the twenty-dollar bills, the official casually noted that the tournament had picked up the tab for the airfares of some of the amateur players like Marita Redondo. The reason was twofold: the tournament committee felt Marita would be a good drawing card, and besides, since she could not accept prize money—say $1,200 if she were a semifinalist—the tournament would still be saving money when it bought her a $300 round-trip ticket from California. Another official told me that when an amateur won a tournament, the fact that she couldn't accept the first-prize money often saved the event from

101

bankruptcy. As Marilyn Fernberger had suggested, women's tennis was still in the minor leagues when it came to tournament financing.

Helga folded the bills into her purse as we drove to the Albermarle. Her prize money on the tour, about $5,000, was no great shakes to her; she had won as much in a single tournament in the past. Now, after eight weeks on the road, all she wanted to do was to get back to her husband in Germany: "He is not zo happy about zo much travel," she said.

The tiny room at the Albermarle that she shared with another player was a mess. "I expected to beat ze Czech girl von-und-love; I didn't bozzer to pack," Masthoff said as she threw underwear into a large suitcase with one hand and sipped from a bottle of club soda in the other. It was not a new routine for her. Helga had a reputation for booking dozens of airline flights every place she went, so she could leave at will. Here in St. Petersburg, she had a reservation on a flight the next day, but not today, and I didn't understand how she hoped to get on a plane for New York at the last minute. I would soon find out.

Quickly but not too efficiently, Masthoff filled one large suitcase, one big carryall, one overnight bag and a flight bag. Her clothes included two beautiful long dresses and several lovely pairs of slacks that she had not gotten to wear. "Ve sought zey vould have zum evenings planned for us, but zere vas nussing." Leaving two little just-rinsed socklets drying on the bathroom doorknobs, we both sat on the large suitcase until Helga snapped it shut. No one was around to help us drag the luggage plus Helga's six Lacoste metal racquets, two jackets and purse out to the car. Whatever glamor there was in a tennis player's world seemed very far away.

I sped toward the Tampa airport with Masthoff grumbling all the way. The Florida weather had been so terrible —"Oh, the heat, you feel as though you are dying." The players had been tougher than she expected—"All zose young vons . . . sixteen, seventeen, and all zo good.

Aggh!" We made it to the terminal with ten minutes
to spare. Leaving her bags in the trunk, Helga calmly presented her ticket for the next day to the reservations clerk.
"I'm on the five o'clock to New York. My bags are checked,"
she lied. She returned to the car to collect her luggage. "I
do it all ze time," she said smiling craftily. "Ze ticket is
for ze exact same flight tomorrow. Zey never bozzer to
check za date!"

By Saturday, the Everts and Evonne were just about
the only show left at Bartlett Park. Chris had beaten Navratilova and Evonne had downed Redondo in the semifinals
to set up the third straight "Ev and Chrissie" final, while
the Evert sisters were about to surprise themselves by
reaching the doubles final against Goolagong and Young
as well. First, however, they had to get past Sharon Walsh
and Patti Hogan, one of the more experienced doubles
pairs among the women pros.

In the lounge before that doubles, it was summer
camp again. Jeanne sat around joking with friends, Chris
sat around joking with reporters, Patti tried to find someone to pick up a jacket for her at a nearby tailor shop.
Finally Jeanne asked Chris cheerfully, "Well, we gonna
play these guys?" and the four of them walked out onto the
court. I commented to a tour official that the four of them
looked as if they were going out for a picnic rather than a
tennis match. He shook his head. "If it's anything like
Sarasota, it could be a doosy. That one got pretty vicious,"
he said ominously. What made it vicious? "Patti Hogan's
behavior," he replied.

The Everts, underdogs for a change, were loose and
even a little showboaty, with Chris gaily waving a racquet
over her head after missing a lob, Jeanne first falling down
on a point, then jumping up with a "Yay!" after Chris had
saved the point. As the Everts drew ahead in the first set,
5-4, Sharon and Patti grew sour. On the final point of the
tenth game, Patti double-faulted, Chris blurted "Out" as
the ball went by, and Flo Blanchard, in the umpire's chair,

103

followed with her own "Out" call. Hogan, eyes blazing, swiveled toward the chair. "You have a linesman to call it!" she yelled. "I called it out," the older woman answered. "Yeah, after Chris and Jeanne talked you into it!" Flo ignored her, announcing, "Game, and first set to the Everts." Chris and Jeanne whispered together, then giggled as they came to the sidelines.

The second set went to Hogan and Walsh, although Jeanne, supposedly the weakest of the four players, hung in gamely as Patti and Sharon worked on her at the net. I was intrigued, having come to know the four of them, by the emotions flicking back and forth, unspoken, as the match progressed. Chris, the stern older sister, would glare tight-lipped at Jeanne when the younger girl made an error, yet carefully announce "Good one!" when Jeanne hit a winner. Sharon laughed pityingly at herself as she started to miss easy shots in the third set, while Patti concentrated on staring down spectators who applauded her errors. The Everts were using all their powers of concentration to keep themselves from being distracted by their opponents. But there was no question that like the proper young women they were, Chris and Jeanne were disgusted by the spectacle of those two disheveled creatures spilling their messy emotions all over the court. The Everts took the third set 6-0. At the end, the four barely shook hands at the net, Jeanne muttered, "It's horrible to play those two," and Patti stormed off to the dressing room, leaving a trail of "Motherfucker" in her wake. I felt as though I had not watched a tennis match, but a group therapy session.

By finals time Sunday afternoon, Bartlett Park had a standing room only crowd of about 4,500 customers, most of them elderly couples or young girls. Chris Evert (and Jimmy Evert) had been shrewd to choose the U.S.L.T.A. tour, I decided. They knew very well that, especially after the pullout of Virginia Wade, the competition would not be strong until the finals each week. This was training for the big tournaments of Europe coming up, a series of work-outs and wind sprints. Vic Edwards, I assumed, had chosen the same route for the same reason for his client. Indeed, by the end of the summer, Chris reflected thoughtfully on how she had paced herself while the Slims women had worn themselves out on a thirteen-week grind.

Flo Blanchard, who umpired matches without pay, was sitting in the lounge wondering who was going to volunteer for line judging that day. The low quality of linesmen and umpires at so many matches could be attributed again to a carryover from amateur days. Almost all were local tennis association officials, club members or hangers-on who did line judging for kicks. Mrs. Blanchard was a professional, even without a salary, and it bothered her to see loosely called matches. Thus today, she asked Jane "Deedee" Dalley, an intense young woman who was a well-trained itinerant linesman, if she would be the net judge for the finals. "The others don't know what 'not ups' are," Mrs. Blanchard said resignedly.*

Deedee suggested adding a foot-fault judge as well; she had noticed that Chris had been foot-faulting consistently through the tournament. Flo did not want to risk foot-fault calls with amateur linesmen. "Besides, Chrissie doesn't rush the net, so what does it really matter?"

At 2:30 P.M., the two finalists strolled out onto the court, each cradling several racquets in her arms, Chris in powder blue, Evonne in white. One of the pleasures of women's tennis was the contrast that singles opponents often presented in looks, style and attitude, a contrast I often found lacking in the men's game. It was something like seeing a prizefight with a bantamweight going against a light-heavy, or a football game with a speedy flanker one-on-one against a guard. Here, it was fair skin versus olive; a long, straight ponytail versus a mass of curls; a gliding, bouncing skater versus a steady, monotonous runner.

---

* When a player hits a ball after it has bounced twice, it is "not up" and her opponent wins the point.

Evonne was more than merely graceful, she was the most fluid player I'd ever watched, the racquet an extension of her arm, her body so flexible there didn't seem to be any bones in it. She played with a half smile on her lips, whisking crosscourt backhands the way lifeguards flick towels at flies on the beach.

But with all her balletic grace, Evonne's game came alive only sporadically in the first set as Chris broke her serve three times to win 6-2. In the second set, Evonne's first serve suddenly improved dramatically and with it her confidence. Calm, steady Chris watched with dismay as Goolagong, whom Patti Hogan wryly called "not one of your great percentage players," hit winner after winner, dropshots and backhand drives, reeling off six straight games to take the set at love.

The crowd, pleased at getting its money's worth, cheered both girls equally and lustily. It might be "Chrissie country," but as Chris was to learn all summer long, tennis crowds always rooted for the underdog, even if she was playing against Florida's most successful homegrown product since oranges. Moreover, Evonne had the flash, the spark, while Chris's fire was hidden in the laser-like concentration that put her, as if by magic, exactly in perfect position to hit practically every ball nearly every time. What amazed me about Chris's game—and it took months of watching her to appreciate it—was that *she* had the radar-accuracy on her strokes, not Evonne. She was a thinking player who was always pushing, pushing, pushing her opponents, first to one corner, then to the other, bringing them in if they were slow-footed so she could then loop a pinpoint lob just beyond their reach or shoot a perfectly placed passing shot down the line. "Chris plays points like a siege war in the Middle Ages," said Julie Heldman.

Chris the Steady, Evonne the Lily Maid. The final set began evenly enough. But Goolagong, her strenuous serve and volley work taking its toll on her in the heat, fell behind 3-1, then 4-1, then 5-1. Just when it seemed as though

106

Chris had only to wait for Evonne to finish herself off on her own serve, the Australian girl caught fire again. She picked up ten straight points, fought off a match point and drove the crowd wild with anticipation as she reached 4-5 before Chris stamped out the flames. The siege was over; the Lily Maid's pretty castle once more overrun.

Evonne received prolonged applause, which grew into a standing ovation as she was announced as the winner of the week's "sportsmanship trophy." Chris graciously accepted the winner's check, but her mind was already working on the next piece of business, the doubles final. As the two girls were led into the lounge for the post-match interview, Conley announced they'd both have a half-hour's rest before joining Janet Young and Jeanne on the court again. "Tell you what," Evonne said to Chris with an exhausted smile, "let's have the other two play each other and we'll watch."

"I default," agreed Chris, joking, as she sank into an easy chair. (The Everts later beat Goolagong and Young in the doubles final.)

I was impressed by the way both Chris and Evonne had handled themselves; it seemed rather marvelous that both kept the tensions of a grueling three-set final in check. But in the corridor near the locker room I saw at last that even Chris was human. Colette Evert, a friendly, frank woman who enjoyed her daughter's star status but displayed none of the neurotic egotism of stage mothers, was standing with Chris and Jeanne when Evonne passed by. Seeing her, Colette remarked lightly, "You played a great match, Evonne. Don't worry, you'll catch Chrissie one of these days. You'll probably get her at Wimbledon!"

Goolagong, embarrassed, looked at Chris and asked incredulously, "Is this your *mother?*" Chris said nothing. Her face was ashen. She whirled, cast a withering glance at Mrs. Evert, blurted "Mom!" as if it were a curse, and stalked off. Miss American Pie might look like your basic ingenue, but underneath was an icy competitor's determination that blew up when someone kidded about the biggest tournament of them all.

The Everts were still in the lounge when I strolled into the locker room for a last look around. Chris had left her tennis carryall in there, her street clothes spread out over a couch, her Wilson racquets casually piled on the floor. The only person in the room was a little ball girl. The sight of her there would remain with me for a long time. She was about ten years old, her long straight blonde hair parted in the middle and pulled into a ponytail at the neck just like Chris's. She was standing all by herself in a green tournament T-shirt, silently sweeping one of Chris's racquets back and forth in the arc of a two-fisted backhand.

Wimbledon

World Series

WIMBLEDON: THE BRITISH UTTERED THE THREE SYLLABLES in the same reverent tones they used for "Trafalgar." It didn't exactly send shivers up my spine, but it did send them up the spines of many players and, if one were to judge by the London newspapers, most of the British race.

"So you're here for the big one," a British tennis writer said to me at the mammoth dinner party in the Savoy Hotel that ushered in the first Wimbledon week. "Now you'll see what tennis is all about. No commercials here!" He chuckled.

"Listen," Julie Heldman confided as we sat down at a table to eat our roast beef, "this is the *old* number. Amateursville. You'll see. Tea and crumpets, stiff upper lip, God save the Queen. You'll love it. But don't let it fool you."

Kids who want to be baseball or football players grow up with the dream of playing in the World Series or the Super Bowl. Kids who want to be tennis players dream of Wimbledon. For the women and the men pros, all the tournaments leading up to the fortnight at the end of June were spring training, all those afterward nice exhibitions. At least, that was the general attitude for nearly a century after the first Men's Championship was held at the All-England Club on the outskirts of London in 1877.

With the coming of the big money in tennis in the 1970's the overpowering influence of Wimbledon was declining, however imperceptibly. The prize money ($12,500 for the men's singles winner, $7,500 for the women's) was piddling now compared to the $50,000 given the World Championship Tennis (men's) playoff winner and the $30,000 given the Sea Pines Family Circle Cup (women's) winner, not to mention the $25,000 top prizes to be awarded later in the year at the U. S. Open at Forest Hills. The players grumbled about the old-fashioned rules (no colored clothing, no tie breaker in the final set of a match), the lack of practice time, the preferential treatment given British players, the scarcity of complimentary tickets. More importantly, for the second year in a row, in 1973, the men's competition at Wimbledon was going to be a devalued one. In a dispute with the international tennis establishment over the suspension of Nikki Pilic, a Yugoslavian pro, eighty-two of the top men players in the world were boycotting the tournament. (The previous year, a slew of the top men had been barred because they held contracts with W.C.T.)

The great spectacle was about to be carried on, regardless. "This is one of the great social occasions of England," Ann Haydon Jones, the former champion-turned-sportscaster, said later in the week. "That's why the men failed to kill it. This is the place to be this fortnight; anyone who is anybody comes here. Britain is still so very hidebound by its traditions, but there is also something very lovely about the traditions. Of course some still like to think we made a mistake allowing Open tennis in 1968. The people here still think there's something nasty about professional sports."

With only a few exceptions, the British newspaper tennis writers pilloried the boycotters in print, castigating them as money-mad mutineers when in fact they were simply trying to wrest a small percentage of control in their profession from a ruling class that treated them like serfs. The papers laid most of the blame at the feet of American promoters like Jack Kramer ("The Week the U. S. Dollar Smiled" was the headline in one newspaper, which was amusing considering the dollar was taking a beating on international money markets that week) and asserted that the greatness of Wimbledon as an institution would survive such petty squabbles. Meanwhile, the press largely ignored another side of the story, which was that for the second year in a row the great challenges of the sport would occur in the women's competition, where the Slims and the U.S.-L.T.A. players would be playing in the same draw for the first time that season.

Writing about Wimbledon several years ago, Paul E. Deutschman noted that it was "the most satisfactory occasion for an American to view the British at their most British," a "testament to the unmatchable British talent for combining judicious portions of drama, pageantry and the game-for-the-game's sake." For me, it was an occasion to see them also at their most snobbish and sexiest.

The day before the tournament began, the Sunday *Times* of London had a rundown on the leading players. The story on the men was a straightforward "who's who"; the column on the women was in the form of a horoscope. ("Imaginative, sensitive," it said of Virginia Wade; "restless and sensuous" of Chris Evert.) It was not the "women's" championships in the official program, but the "ladies'," not "Billie Jean King" but "Mrs. L. W. King." With typical chauvinism, the British seemed to have forgotten that modern lawn tennis was a sport invented, in 1874, by their own countryman, Major Walter C. Wingfield, specifically for the ladies of his castle, who wanted an outdoor sport that would give them more exercise than croquet. (In fact, the histories showed women also pioneered in tennis in the United States. The first matches ever played in the stadium at Forest Hills were a women's Wightman Cup series in 1923.) Now, nearly a century later, Ann Jones, the 1969 women's singles winner, an Englishwoman herself, did television commentary for the B.B.C. only on women's matches, and only those on Court One: "I'm not allowed on Centre Court yet. It's accepted that men can comment on women's matches but not that women can comment on men's."

But at Wimbledon, there was class chauvinism to

113

match the male chauvinism. Inside the famed Centre Court, the Royal Box featured upholstered green lawn chairs, and there were more than 10,000 seats for the bourgeoisie, all of them reserved at prices starting at £2 ($5), while 3,000 peons, many of whom waited in overnight queues at the gates, were forced to stand in uncovered sun-baked stone tiers on either side of the stadium. There were separate toilets under the Centre Court stands for All-England Club members, plus a separate members' luncheon garden that was as off limits to players and press as it was to the peons. (One day Edy McGoldrick, a member, told me to look for her in the luncheon enclosure. When, press pass in hand, I told the guard at the gate I wanted to step inside to find her, he shoved me away. "If the lady had wanted to see you, she would have left your name," he announced.) By comparison, Forest Hills was a hotbed of Communism.

Even so, there was an undeniable majestic excitement about the scene as the week began. The windows of Harrod's were decorated with Teddy Tinling tennis dresses designed especially for Wimbledon. The disk jockeys on Radio One, the B.B.C. rock station, chatted about the upcoming matches in between songs. At the Sunday night party, Billie Jean, looking slim and ladylike in a long skirt, circulated from table to table on the arm of her husband, like the sport's own version of Elizabeth and Philip. The next morning, the Underground trains to Southfields (the Wimbledon subway stop) were packed with eager fans carrying picnic hampers. "We live in the country," a matron in a flowery hat told me as we piled into a cab for the five-minute ride to the club, "but we *always* have a box at Wimbledon."

I had no box, no ticket, no credentials, and for the next two weeks I felt like a cub reporter from Podunk suddenly assigned to New York's Shea Stadium for a World Series. I knew exactly three people in the huge international press corps, two of whom were Marilyn and Ed Fernberger, who had wangled press badges as part-time photographer and writer for *World Tennis* magazine. Not that it mattered. Wimbledon press passes were rationed as rigidly as sugar cubes in World War Two by a wall-eyed, bulbous-nosed old hack named Roy McKelvie, who made it a point to insult as many writers as he could during his brief reign in the All-England Club pressroom each year. McKelvie, who held the job as press chief despite an obvious conflict of interest (he wrote for the Sunday *Express* and a British tennis magazine), allotted only one Centre Court pass to each newspaper, one each to selected other media people, none to me and a host of other unlucky novices. (A major American magazine bribed a tournament official $1,000 to get a badge for its reporter.) *The New York Times* stringer for the event gave me a "messenger" pass which let me onto the club grounds, but for the rest of the week I had to beg, borrow and buy seats if I wanted to see the Centre Court action.

My trials, however, were no worse than those of some of the players. On the first day of women's singles matches, Tory Fretz scored a minor upset by knocking out Linda Mottram, the sixteen-year-old daughter of a well-known English coach and a prospect highly touted by the British press. "I made sure I beat her good," said Tory with a defiant look when I ran into her in the daily jam of players and spectators in the main concrete walk between Centre Court and the side courts. Over dinner the following night, she explained why.

Despite a decent record on the Slims tour that spring and a Number 12 ranking among U. S. women in 1972, she had been refused direct entry in the ninety-six-player draw and forced to play three preliminary rounds to qualify. "They told me my record wasn't good enough, even though I had wins against five of the players in the draw," she said angrily. "That's pretty hard to take. Don't let anybody tell you being a tennis pro's a picnic."

Even a picnic would have been no picnic for Tory Fretz. She was one of those people for whom life was a psychological mine field. A month away from her thirty-first birthday, she had never worked in anything else but tennis except for a brief stint as a salesgirl in Bullock's. Originally

115

from Harrisburg, Pennsylvania, she had developed into a promising junior. She was accompanied to tournaments by an overprotective mother who watched her like a hawk on the court, at meals, in the locker room shower. She had moved to Los Angeles, studied under Alice Marble, had a romance with the actor Efrem Zimbalist, Jr., gotten as high as a Number 4 U. S. ranking one year, gone through psychoanalysis, and nearly crippled herself attempting to play with a torn knee cartilage.

For Tory, as for many of the players, each match was a battle against herself as much as it was against an opponent. She had a good, aggressive all-around game and knew how to exploit other players' weaknesses, but she would choke at crucial points; despite years of match play, she just wasn't tough enough against an opponent she knew was better than she. At least, not when it counted.

"I'm the world's greatest practice player," she said once after beating Billie Jean in a friendly game when the only thing at stake was a haircut from Billie Jean's secretary, which King had promised her if she won. Another time, after she had taken the first set from someone and then lost the match, a friend remarked, "Maybe Tory got scared she'd win."

I liked Tory immensely—she was as good-natured and affectionate as a sheepdog, a person who was so kindhearted she often wound up having dinner or having a hit with people she knew were taking advantage of her—and it hurt me to listen to her replay every bad shot when she lost. "Couldn't get my first serve in . . . that damn dropshot. . . . Jeez, I'm really down . . . had her 4-2 in the second. . . ." Same old story.

Now she was back at Wimbledon trying, as so many of the fringe players were, to combat not just herself but the obstacles that being a fringe player had put in her path. She had arrived in London a few weeks before on a delayed flight from Los Angeles, expecting to rest for a day or two before playing the pre-Wimbledon tournaments at Nottingham and Queen's Club. Instead, her roommate informed

her as she checked into her hotel at 4 A.M. that she had
been assigned a match that afternoon in Nottingham, three
hours away, that she had not been put in the main Wimbledon draw and that as a qualifier she would not get a free
room for the Wimbledon fortnight at the Gloucester, the
official players' hotel. "I was ready to get on the next plane
home, but I couldn't even do that because I was on a
twenty-two-day excursion ticket!" she said, sighing.

Most of that was now behind her; she was pleased that
she had survived the pressure of qualifying and she was
comfortably ensconced in the Gloucester, registered under
the name of Rosie Casals, who had gotten her an extra
room. But the pressure would not go away, not until she
lost, at any rate. "I get so damn nervous!" she said over
dinner in a little Italian restaurant where I drank all the
wine. "Mental concentration—that's what makes all the
difference. The Old Lady has it, right up here." She pointed
at her head. I asked for her expert opinion on who would
take the women's crown this year. "The Old Lady," she
repeated. "She's up for it."

The Gloucester, a spanking-new, American-style luxury hotel in the Kensington section of London twenty
minutes by tube from Wimbledon, was in-town headquarters for the players and the hangers-on. The tournament
was the hotel's initial public relations gambit and its shake-
down cruise. It had invited all the players and members of
the press to try out the facilities before the first actual paying guests did a week later. Each day the lobby swarmed
with young men and women in warm-up suits, waiting for
rides in the official white British Leyland tournament cars
to either Queen's Club, where practice sessions were held,
or to the All-England Club itself.

The hotel was also the place for players' association
meetings, business conferences with agents and sponsors,
after-hours drinking. (Its bar remained open long after the
pubs were closed.) Billie Jean King had just formed a
union of the women players, the Women's Tennis Associa-

117

tion, and its first meetings were held in a Gloucester banquet room that week. They lasted for hours (with Billie Jean, the president, presiding) and soon the women started grumbling that they were going to lose their muscle tone from sitting around so much. But while others staggered out of the meetings bleary-eyed (they were closed to the press), King seemed refreshed by them.

Early in the first week, I caught her after a meeting to introduce myself and arrange for an interview. "Oh, you're doing a book!" she said brightly. "So am I. What's yours about? Who's your publisher?" She playfully grabbed my pencil and pretended to take notes. "Maybe I should interview you!" She laughed. At her side, looking pale and waiflike, was Marilyn Barnett, who fished a piece of paper out of her Gucci attaché case (a gift from a boyfriend) and made a note to add me to Billie Jean's busy schedule. "She likes to have set routines," Marilyn noted in her Baby Doll voice. Marilyn, who was twenty-five, had been a Hollywood hairdresser until this year, when Billie Jean had signed her on as personal secretary, traveling companion and high priestess of the Billie Jean sect of worshipful admirers. A wispy flower-child of a woman with streaky blonde hair who favored print halter-dresses, Marilyn knew almost nothing about tennis ("I'm learning—I know what 15, 30, 40 means now"), had difficulty spelling and would have looked more at home on a hippie commune than in a locker room. Billie Jean had hired her not so much for her business skills but because she liked to have Marilyn around. Marilyn spent far more time with her than Larry, Billie Jean's husband, did. She bought her clothes, kept her appointment book, chauffeured her and acted as all-around lady's maid. They were a strange, totally contradictory, but apparently very compatible pair, with Marilyn effectively shielding Billie Jean from intruders she didn't want to be bothered with. The relationship could take on ominous shades: at Forest Hills later in the year, Marilyn accidentally dropped a handful of pre-autographed index cards and

Billie Jean, who was in a bad mood, ordered her from between clenched teeth, "Pick those up. Now!" One reporter, a witness, described it as a scene right out of *The Killing of Sister George.* In general, however, Marilyn's imperturbable calm seemed made to order to complement Billie Jean's effervescence.

When not by Billie Jean's side, Marilyn was usually seated in the players' tearoom, the competitors' unofficial headquarters at Wimbledon. One flight above a large refreshment stand, with bay windows facing the big wood scoreboard that listed who was playing or had finished playing on every court, the tearoom was a noisy, crowded, cheerful jumble of glass tables and white wicker chairs where the players gathered before and after matches to get a free meal (they had chits for lunch and tea each day), to gossip, to drink at the bar, to watch the side courts from the rooftop patio or to watch the telecast of the Centre Court matches on the big color TV in the bar lounge.

The players had much to talk about. The Slims circuit had ended the first week in May with a smashing victory by Rosie Casals over Nancy Richey Gunter in the Family Circle Cup at Sea Pines, South Carolina, for $30,000— the biggest prize ever awarded in women's sports. During May and June, many players had rested while others had played a string of tournaments in Europe. But by far the most significant match of the late spring had not been part of a tournament. It was the Mother's Day Massacre, in which Margaret Court had embarrassed herself and a million other women by losing 6-2, 6-1 to Bobby Riggs.

Linda Tuero sat near a window the afternoon of the first day of women's play (the women's singles matches were played every other day) with a glum look on her small, cheerleader-pretty face. The twenty-one-year-old Louisianan, a clay-court specialist, had just been upset in the first round on the slick Wimbledon grass by an unheralded Frenchwoman. "I'd kill her on anything else!

Kill her!" she was telling a group of friends, including Chris Evert. "It's so depressing, this damn surface. I can't get my footwork. I had no confidence, then I started missing, and I guess I got thoroughly depressed. Deep in my subconscious, I wanted to lose. I unpacked my bags last night for the first time and I guess I really was thinking of going home. After traveling for so long you just get—ugh!" she concluded. Chris nodded in sympathy; she was having similar problems.

For many of the American players, the European circuit, as Tuero indicated, was more of a pain in the neck than a Grand Tour. They were used to having everything arranged for them by either the Slims or the U.S.L.T.A.— housing, meals, parties, practice. In Europe, they had to do it themselves. They were accustomed to private homes or Holiday Inns; in Europe, they had to deal with concierges. Both Linda and Chris complained about the language difficulties. Linda recalled a tour stop one year in Naples: "It was awful. There was no hot water at the hotel. They kept on saying, '*Domani, domani.*' By the time I left I thought I was on the verge of a breakdown."

Some players, the more adventurous and sophisticated ones, had gone on the international circuit in past years precisely because it gave them a chance to see the world. Julie Heldman, for instance, returned to tennis in 1968 after quitting two years earlier because she wanted to travel. By 1970, she had gone to the Caribbean twice, South Africa, Rome, Paris, London, Buenos Aires, Santiago, Tel Aviv, Moscow and Cleveland, among other places. "It was a kind of freedom," she said. "In '69 I was Number 5 in the world, I did fabulously well in the Caribbean, I would go out and party, I was fit, and everything was lovely. But I realized pretty soon that what I was doing there was simply being a pawn for the rich, for people who paid for the little tickets and came out and saw you dashing around, and then patted you on the head at parties. I didn't mind if I got a free trip some place and made money to boot. But there was no reason why they should get me cheap—and boy, was I going for cheap in '69. $150 a week."

Chris listened to most of the conversation with Linda Tuero without saying a word. It had been a disconcerting month for her. On the spring tour in the U. S., she had lost only once in forty-seven matches. Now, she was in a slump, the first she'd ever suffered. "I'm learning what it means to lose," she said ruefully. Her European tour had started off well enough in France and Italy, and she got to the finals of the Italian Championship in Rome. But there, for the first time ever on clay, she lost to Evonne. The next tournament she lost the final to Margaret Court, again on clay, after being up one set and 5-3 in the second, serving for the match, two points from victory.

Then came England, grass, disaster. She had been knocked out of three tournaments in a row by players she had never lost to, the last one Julie Heldman at Queen's the week before. Her mother was with her, but they were barely speaking, to hear Colette tell it. Jimmy Connors, her boyfriend, was there, but he couldn't play her matches for her. At Queen's, after the loss to Heldman, she had walked over to the first bench she could find and cried. The Ice Dolly was melting.

She got little sympathy from her fellow pros. At the St. Petersburg tournament two months before, I had watched as other players, especially the foreigners, rooted for Chris to lose. "I've seen it before," Flo Blanchard said. "It was the same with Maureen Connolly—the golden girl. Nobody likes the one on top." Now, the same players were taking quiet satisfaction in Chris the Steady's shakiness. "Overrated all along," declared one of the Slims women. "Get her on grass and she doesn't know what to do."

The Slims didn't bother to conceal the fact that their antipathy to Chris stemmed as much from her status as a loner as from what they felt was her limited skill. "If it hadn't been for us, there would never have been a U.S.L.T.A.

121

tour in the first place, with that kind of money," said Rosie Casals. "We created women's tennis, we created the future for Chris Evert. When she signed with the U.S.L.T.A., she gave us a kick in the mouth."

Even the spectators were less than entranced with the Ice Dolly. "I wish she'd *smile* more," said one middle-aged lady as she watched Chris struggle to beat a Peruvian player, Fiorella Bonicelli, in the first round. There was no reason to smile. Julie Heldman lay in wait for her in the third round, anxious to prove her Queen's Club victory was no fluke.

Julie M.

THE TENSION GENERATED BY WIMBLEDON WAS PALPABLE; I could see it in the grim mask of Chris's face, in the slow, deliberate steps Margaret Court took as she climbed the stairs each day to the ladies' locker room, in Julie Heldman's voice as she brushed by me one day after a match, saying, "We'll talk after my Evert thing—I'm not speaking, not *thinking* about anything else till then."

The match was just that—an Evert thing. As the first set began on Centre Court, Chris looked nervous and tentative, hanging back at her beloved baseline, losing her first service game on a double-fault. But Heldman was twice as nervous. At 3-2, advantage Heldman on her own serve, Julie threw away a chance to move firmly into the lead by double-faulting.

Tennis, Neil Amdur, the *Times* sportswriter, had told me time and again, was a game of levels. An inferior player could take a set from a better player, and sometimes a match, by raising her game to her opponent's level for sustained periods, even when all the statistics proved on paper that it couldn't happen. The players called it "playing out of your tree"—the shots just came, like manna from heaven, reinforcing the player's confidence, pushing the level of her game still higher. Then, when both levels were even, one crucial point—a ball that hit the net cord and dribbled over to the other side, an unbelievable passing shot that caught the chalk—could either put the match in one player's pocket or destroy the other's concentration.

Neil insisted that because the women had a slower, more mental game than the men, and thus because women had to fight harder than men to maintain their match play concentration, there was almost always one game, one point, which an experienced observer could immediately detect as the turning point of a match. This was why, he said, the scores of so many women's matches showed the winner picking up a second set 6-1 or 6-0 after a close first set. "Poof—after the crucial point comes, the match is really over, no matter what the scoreboard shows," he had argued.

I wasn't sure that I agreed with him. Chris Evert, to name just one player, consistently fought from behind and came out on top. But in the Heldman-Evert match, Neil's theory seemed to be operating. After the double-fault at 3-2, Julie went steadily downhill. She had an awkward, rather ugly style of play, as if she had an invisible brace on her neck and splints on her forearms—everything about her was stiff. She hit her forehand with her arm crooked in toward her body, her backhand with almost no backswing. It was like seeing a wound-up toy soldier hitting tennis balls. She played with an absolutely fierce scowl of concentration on her face, her eyes scrunched up, her mouth locked in a half-open position that made her prominent teeth seem vampirish, her hair pushed up under a white puffy hat. Poor Julie. As she stood with Chris at the sidelines, the first phrase that came to mind was "Beauty and the Beast." Beauty won, 6-3, 6-1.

A lot of players underwent near-total transformations in appearance when they were off the court. The hair would come tumbling out from buns and ponytails, the headbands would disappear revealing noble foreheads, the match play stare would dissolve into a human face, the thick thighs would be hidden beneath well-tailored slacks. It took me more than a few times to recognize Kristien Kemmer, who parted her hair in the middle and bundled it up for playing, as the lovely young woman with the long streaked hair whom I was always seeing in the tearoom. The transformation of Julie Heldman was even more startling. As we sat down one day on the tearoom roof, I realized that she was quite attractive, with a hoydenish face and high arched eyebrows, a ready smile and a first-rate brain.

"I am Julie M. Heldman, asthmatic, college graduate, writer, broadcaster, tennis player, in that order," she announced. "Some people only hit tennis balls. I take care of my health, take care of my mind, and take care of my body. Nobody goes crazy as quick as I do."

It was a reasonable assessment by the most complex personality in women's tennis, an intellectual among jocks, a New York Jew among sunland *shicksas,* a would-be hippie among straights.

Julie had been around tennis all her life. Her mother was Gladys Heldman, who, besides being the publisher of *World Tennis,* and the most formidable figure in the women's pro world, had been a onetime tournament player herself. Her father, Julius, an oil company executive now based in Houston, was a seniors' champion. Her older sister Trixie competed in a tournament every once in a while too, when she wasn't playing bass guitar with a rock band.

Like a large contingent of the women players, Julie had grown up in a world that revolved around the game. In no other sport except swimming were there so many family combinations—sister teams, brother-sister teams, coach-father-player-child teams—it was one of the factors that made the sport so inbred. The obvious explanation was that recreational tennis was such a family sport that intra-household workouts often led children naturally into competing in junior tournaments and then professional play. "The only way the kids get to see their parents is at the tennis courts," Gladys Heldman said in analyzing the phenomenon of tennis families. "When Julie M. was a little girl, she learned to play because I would tell her, 'If you're good, Mommy will hit with you.' "

At the turn of the century, the four Sutton sisters from Santa Monica started the phenomenon. For a time they so

dominated a local tournament that someone suggested re-
naming it the "Sutton California Championships." Later
came the Richeys—sister Nancy, brother Cliff, and father-
coach George—then the Everts. The current women's circuit featured four sister duos, the Everts, Laurie and Carrie
Fleming, Laurie and Robin Tenney and the Schwikert twins,
Jill and Joy. Marita Redondo had a younger brother and
sister coming up fast in the juniors and there were a host of
lesser families too. "Yeah, they're popping up in pairs these
days, aren't they?" said Julie Heldman. "It's bad enough
with one Evert, but when you know there are three more
waiting in line . . ."

Julie might have been born into tennis, but she spent
critical moments in her life trying to get away from it. She
had done well in the juniors, done well in college (a history
degree with honors from Stanford in 1966), done fairly well
in regular women's competition. She had also started to go
crazy.

"All my life I was programmed to quit," she explained.
"In high school, people said, 'When are you going to quit?'
In college they were saying, 'When are you going to quit?'
Everybody else was going off and doing things, and I was
going off and hitting tennis balls. I just thought I would play
to a certain age and then quit and get married and have
children. Nobody I knew—boy or girl—continued to play
after age nineteen. If you could play just in college that was
good enough. By '66, I was having no fun at all. You could
see it in me on the court. The pain was written right across
my face. I had started college when I was sixteen, so not
only did I push my tennis career, but I pushed my education. When I was about to finish college in 1966, there really
was very little to look forward to. I had come to the limit
of my own little tennis game; I wasn't improving. And if
the whole venture of life was to be either the champion or
be married, I was going to get out of there quick. I quit
forever."

For a year, to be exact. During it, Julie, like Margaret
Court, took an excursion into the non-jock world and found

it wanting. Margaret had quit the same year to run a dress
shop in Perth because she was tired of living out of suitcases. Both were fleeing the pressure of competition. Both
ultimately found they missed it.

Julie described her odyssey, sitting on the tearoom
roof, with great verve, the way travelers who have returned
from a frightening sailing trip in rough seas tell about theirs.
"I hardly touched a racquet for a year," she began. "First
I worked for my mother—she was training me to take over
the magazine. And I discovered that if you work the way
my mother does, you work often twenty-four hours at a
stretch, which wasn't exactly where I was at. Then I finished
my last quarter in college, and then I went and lived in the
hills of northern California with my sister and a hippie rock
and roll band. Then I went back to New York, where my
mother's best friend got me a job as a secretary in the
Art Department at Wells, Rich, Greene. I was the wildest
thing they'd ever seen, but I mean, I was determined that
if I was going to do anything, I would do it the way I was
supposed to. I was there from bloody nine to bloody five
every day. I used to envy the message boy because at least
he got out in the street. I lasted three months. One day I
had a revelation from the stars that it was time for me to
go. I took off on a trek with some friends across America
and camped out."

Finally, she wound up at Dennis van der Meer's tennis
camp, got a job teaching, and discovered that tennis could
be fun if it wasn't one's whole existence. She enjoyed the
"shamateur" life, enjoyed being a pro when Open tennis
came along even more. But there would always be a basic
conflict in Julie. She defined it by saying, "I have a sort of
amateur spirit about me from time to time. I like to enjoy
myself, to meet people. The tour becomes a grind in America. I'm supposed to be a professional, but it still becomes
a grind." There was more to it than that. Julie knew there
was a real world outside the tennis world, and she wanted
to be totally involved in both. So she wrote magazine articles—tough, perceptive ones—about her colleagues for

World Tennis and other publications. The most recent was a bitchy piece on Chris Evert for the London Sunday *Times Magazine*—"Miss Evert is eighteen and the most carefully packaged commercial property in the world of sport"—which appeared at the start of the fortnight and which Chris refused to read. Julie hung out with writers and artists, did some television commentary.

Another player, Julie Anthony, later spoke of "tunnel vision" as one quality a player needed to climb to the top. Julie Heldman's mind, it seemed to me, was not narrow enough to make her Number 1, even if her tennis skill had been sharper. Ceci Martinez, another bright player, was in somewhat the same predicament. "Some of the other players never read the papers, they never read a book," she said. "I'm always on head trips. Most of the players don't even think about what they're doing in a match. I'm always thinking about it, intellectualizing it. Maybe I'd be better off if I didn't!"

Julie Heldman would probably be better off, too, as a tennis player. But she wouldn't be half as interesting.

Julie stretched out her legs and flexed her left knee. "Nobody gets sick as quick as I do, either," she said, proceeding to catalog the ailments that had plagued her career: recurring bouts with the flu, pneumonia, tennis elbow, a knee operation. She was wearing a dress and I could see two small vertical scars on the knee, the same scars Billie Jean King and Tory Fretz had on theirs. Knee injuries frightened tennis players as much as they did Joe Namath. They could mean the end of a player's mobility, the ruin of a promising career. Tory had had two operations the previous year; the first hadn't worked. Both times she had wound up in a cast from thigh to toes. "They told me I wouldn't be able to play tennis again, and the tears came," she recalled. Tory started going to a physical therapist anyway, but almost quit because she was sure her career had been botched on the operating table. Only when the therapist offered to work with her without charge did she become convinced she might recover. She traveled with a "space boot"—a weighted shoe that she spent half an hour each day with doing leg-lifting exercises.

Billie Jean talked little about her knees, yet when she accidentally strained one of them in New Jersey in August during practice, tripping on the edge of a piece of carpet on the side of the court, she immediately pulled out of the tournament, sent for a doctor, and then went to New York to see Namath's doctor, James Nicholas. Soon she was lifting weights too, telling any reporter who would listen, with somewhat perverse pride, that Dr. Nicholas had diagnosed her knee problems as exactly like Broadway Joe's. She rarely bothered to mention that her knees ached after every match so badly she felt as if she had just played three quarters against the Colts, or that she did calisthenic exercises every morning.

Knee problems were ailments common to both men and women players, of course. Menstrual cramps were literally the curse of the women's circuit. Wendy Overton, among others, admitted she hated to play on the first day of her period. When I asked Julie Heldman about it, she said her period usually didn't bother her; "Your adrenalin usually pumps the cramps out of you." But she pointed out that years ago, there had been a famous instance of a match temporarily suspended for a Tampax break. It was the mixed-doubles final at Wimbledon, when Darlene Hard suddenly ran off the court. "You're supposed to say, 'Excuse me, I need to change my underwear,' or 'I have to go to the toilet,' but she didn't," Julie said. "She just went off—twice in the middle of a match. She claims it was running down her legs. She was one of the great gameswomen of all times, so you never knew what to believe." Julie also mentioned that a lot of younger players suddenly became irregular when they first began to travel extensively. Some of them didn't get their periods for an entire year. "It happened to me when I was nineteen," she said.

The women had to contend with other "women's complaints" as well. One American player, overcome with pain from a vaginal infection during a major European tournament just before Wimbledon, had to default in the middle of a match and was rushed to a hospital. Then there were the birth control pill problems. One famous player, a Catholic, went on the pill specifically to regulate her period so she wouldn't have to deal with inopportune cramps during a big match. Others found to their consternation that the pill made them gain weight and brought on uncomfortable breast swelling.

Later in the summer, in New Jersey, the ladies' locker room attendant told me that after Band-Aids, Tampax was the item most in demand during the week. In seven days, the thirty-two players had used up one king-sized box of tampons, three hundred Band-Aids, several bottles of hydrogen peroxide and two fat rolls of surgical tape.

Before we finished our talk on the roof, I asked Julie M. (as her mother invariably referred to her) for her choice to win the women's championship. "Billie Jean, who else?" she said. "You don't bet against Billie Jean at Wimbledon."

Buy Low, Sell High

As THE ROUND OF SIXTEEN—THE ROUND BEFORE THE quarterfinals—began, there had been no major upsets in the women's play. But the trials of Chris Evert were far from over. After Heldman, she was to meet Janet Young, Evonne Goolagong's doubles partner, and Janet, as Evonne informed me outside the tearoom that day, was doing very nicely indeed. "We had to play doubles on Centre Court. It was her first time and I thought she'd be nervous, but she never played so well!"

The Evert-Young match was played on a side court, the bleachers on either side packed with spectators sweating in the unusual 80-degree heat. Chris looked subdued, Janet, determined. Janet felt confident on grass, comfortable in Europe, she had told me. "In America, it's so competitive, you're nothing if you come in Number 2. Here they don't talk about that as much."

Chris did not know what it was like to be Number 2 and as far as Europe was concerned, her visit to the Vatican to see the Pope one Sunday in Rome and her dinner with Jimmy Connors at Maxim's in Paris had not done anything to improve her game. They each took a set, and as I watched Janet storm ahead 3-0 in the third, I realized that my loyalties as a fan were, for the first time, sharply divided. It was no longer a case of observing two tennis players; I *knew* them, had spent time with them, liked them both as people. I wanted Janet to score a stupendous upset, to see her contained elation as she won match point. I wanted Chris to defy the nay-sayers, to pull through her slump by reaching down to the depths of the reserve strength I knew she had in her. I wanted them both to win. I stood on the back step at the top of the bleachers, clutching the railing, as Janet, volleying softly but accurately, fought her way to 4-1, 40-15.

She blew it. Or did she? Chris's cleverly disguised lobs began falling like deadly raindrops—ping, ping, ping— just inside the baseline, as Janet stood flat-footed at the net. 4-2. 4-3. 4-4 . . . 8-6.

Chris was in the quarter finals, and Janet was still a Number 2.

Janet sat in the tearoom, calmly nibbling cheese and crackers. "I couldn't tell she was hitting the lobs until it was too late. 4-1 in the third . . . if I had won that game for 5-1 . . . but then again, that's the sign of a champion, isn't it? You don't deliberately lose. They play better." Janet took a sip of tea. "It's easy to look back. There's little consolation in coming in second."

A chastened Chris Evert sat down at the table with us and they began talking, replaying the big points, second-guessing. "At 15-30 you made an error," Chris said. "You hit a backhand crosscourt you shouldn't have. Remember that?" Janet managed a smile. "No, I don't remember that."

Janet's father, a small gray-haired man who looked more British than Australian, joined them. A management consultant, he made annual trips to Wimbledon, but this was his first with Janet in the draw. "We're very proud of her," he said gently. "Of course, she's not the only athlete in the family. Her twin brother, Colin, is a barefoot water-skier, and her sister, Susan, is an equestrienne."

Janet reported to her father that she had gotten a call after her match the day before, while she was still in the bath, from a young man in Los Angeles she had met during her American spring tour. Her father perked up. "You know," he turned to me, "if you should meet anyone in management consulting you should introduce him to Janet. Or if you meet a tall, dark, handsome man you might introduce him, too." Janet looked vaguely embarrassed. I replied that there was a danger I'd keep the tall, dark, handsome one to myself.

Larry King squatted beside Janet's chair and began giving her a sales pitch for World Team Tennis, a new concept in tennis competition that had been publicly announced a few weeks before. It was to be a league of teams in sixteen American cities that would play a May through July season beginning in 1974. Each team would consist of three women and three men players. King was a founder and vice president. "We'd really like to have you with us," he said earnestly.

Janet's father was a member of one group within the tennis world that coexisted with the players at Wimbledon during the fortnight—the family group. He was among dozens of parents who accompanied their offspring to the championship. King was a member of two groups—family and business. While the players went about their work on the courts each day, these satellite groups swirled around the tearoom and the Gloucester lobby, doing theirs. Here, the parents and husbands functioned less as camp counselors than as intermediaries. Colette Evert, for example, acted basically as Chris's laundress and secretary. ("It's a duty," Colette remarked one day. "I mean, she's paying *my* expenses.")

The British might like to regard Wimbledon as the last stronghold of the amateur spirit, but in reality it was at the same time a mass marketplace of deal-mongers, a teeming tennis medina where the caravans of equipment manufacturers, tournament promoters, dress designers and business managers came once a year to sell their wares and pitch their contracts. The bartering continued, day and night. In the hotel lobby each morning, I would see a Wilson Sporting Goods representative huddled with a player: "I've got to have a pair of shoes." "No problem, come on up to my room." In the tearoom, Owen Williams, a South African tournament promoter: "Wendy, we would enjoy having you in Johannesburg this winter . . . nice hotel, airfare. . . ." One the roof, Jim Hambuechen, one of the leading business agents in women's tennis, bargaining for a better endorsement deal. If Wimbledon had had a coat of arms, its motto would have been "Buy low, sell high."

Hambuechen, a former pro skier, Wall Streeter and advertising man of thirty-eight who had drifted into managing athletes more than a decade earlier, entered the women's field in 1972 after Gladys Heldman told him that almost none of the women players had professional financial advisers. He began with five players—Francoise Durr, Betty Stove, Kerry Melville, Lesley Hunt, Helen Gourlay— then added almost a dozen more within one year. A few dissatisfied clients dropped out before the end of 1973.

Though he did not take a percentage of his clients' prize money, Hambuechen did the players' taxes for a fee, and took a cut from the endorsements he lined up for them. Both he and Larry King, who managed Billie Jean, agreed that women athletes were just beginning to be considered as marketable commodities by the American business world.

"Until three years ago, it would have been impossible to get even tennis equipment endorsements," Larry King told me one day. "In the past, endorsements were usually made through personal contact between an athlete and the chairman of the board or the president of a company. These guys got a kick out of associating with famous stars in football, basketball. They couldn't relate to women as athletic stars."

Billie Jean made the initial breakthroughs, especially with non-tennis products like toothpaste and hair-dryers, but Hambuechen made it clear that other women players still had a long way to go. "Most sponsors say, 'Give me Billie Jean or give me nobody.' It's an educational process we're involved in that's directly related to the importance and size of the women's game."

Even the women who were able to line up endorsements were underpaid and underpromoted by the companies, according to Hambuechen and King. "When I started negotiating racquet contracts, I was met with shocked surprise because of the price I asked," said Jim. "They were really getting ripped off."

Larry King claimed Wilson, each year, underproduced the Billie Jean King model racquets because the company thought only women—still the minority among recreational players—bought them. "There aren't any left in the stores by June," Larry said. "Wilson doesn't think that a man will buy a woman's racquet, but they do it all the time!" (He was absolutely right. In a large New York sporting goods store I noticed a young man paying for three new BJK autograph models and getting a fourth restrung. I remarked on the fact that the sex of the endorser didn't seem to offend him. "It happens to be a great racquet; besides a woman didn't *make* it; she just put her name on it," he replied.)

The business agents found difficulty in getting endorsements for many of the women because so few of them were well-known. Jim Hambuechen lectured his clients on how to develop more public personality; he even went so far as to convince Francoise Durr to have her Airedale terrier, Topspin, carry her racquets onto the court so that people would remember her as "the lady with the dog." Another problem was that certain products, like cosmetics, were items manufacturers believed women athletes could not promote. (Chris Evert was the one player to be offered many "feminine" endorsements—panty hose, soap, and so on—but turned them down on the grounds that posing in the shower, as one company wanted her to do, would be in bad taste. Chris, hardly a feminist, understood commercial sexism to that extent. Or perhaps it was just a case of her basic prudishness.)

Billie Jean, according to Larry, earned in excess of $200,000 in 1972 with half of that coming from endorsements, investments, and business enterprises like Tennis America (a camp franchise). In 1973, with the Riggs match

and its subsequent commercial impact, she made more than
$400,000.

The average woman, as opposed to the top stars, was
lucky to make 15 percent of her yearly income from non-
prize money sources according to Hambuechen.

Both Larry and Jim perceived a not-so-subtle sexism
in the way the women viewed their own business affairs.
"They don't think of themselves in terms of figuring out
what's best for them," Larry said. "They always expect
somebody else to do it: their father, their brother. . . .
They expect some man to do their thinking for them. Billie
Jean is a good student—she does most of her thinking for
herself. But nine times out of ten the women will say, 'Leave
everything to the agent.' A male athlete will let the agent
negotiate, but he'll still know all the details."

Hambuechen acknowledged the same thing, adding that
women, poorly educated about managing money, were
either too cautious or too gullible. One woman, he said, was
conned out of her earnings by a boyfriend. Another had
been investing $50,000 a year in a savings account, even
though she was in such a high tax bracket the government
took most of her interest. "Women in tennis have been ex-
ploited for a long time and they're still too willing to do
favors cheap. They haven't learned to put a value on themselves," said Hambuechen.

For all their business acumen and their seemingly
raised consciousnesses, Hambuechen and King's position
bothered me. Weren't the women falling into the old trap
by having men handle their money? Wouldn't it be more
liberating to have women do that? "Gloria Steinem and that
crew look very askance at the influence I have on Billie
Jean," Larry admitted. "But I think that's chauvinism too.
If a business person has something to offer, you treat him as
an individual whether male or female." Billie Jean took the
same position. After she formed the Women's Tennis Association, the group hired a man, Martin Carmichael, a
lawyer known for his previous affiliation with professional
golfers, as its executive director. When I asked Billie Jean

why the union had not sought out a woman, she replied, to my horror: "You know the answer. We were looking for the most qualified person to do the best possible job, and there were no women available." The Kings did, however, hire a woman as editor of their new sports magazine, *Women Sports*.

In the field of tennis fashions, it had again been a man, Teddy Tinling, who had been more responsible than any woman for liberating female athletes. Teddy was easy to spot at Wimbledon, whether in the tearoom or in the crush of spectators on the narrow walk between the outside courts —he was a head taller than everyone else. Though he may have looked a bit like a creature from outer space, he was completely down to earth when it came to women's tennis. Having made his living from it for forty years, he not only could gab endlessly and interestingly about the sport, its past greats and current stars, but also was a keen, if quirky, student of the women's game. (His theory about Chris Evert's slump, for example, was that because she had shot up several inches in the past year, with most of the growth in her legs, her center of gravity had shifted upward. She had not yet adjusted to the new balance in her body, he claimed.)

The famous lace panties that brought Gussie Moran notoriety in 1951 had been Teddy's creation. The sensation they caused might not have anything to do with lobs or backhands but they had focused welcome attention on women's tennis. "I put sin into tennis," Teddy said proudly. "Tennis couldn't finance itself purely as a sport. It had to turn into a spectacle, and you must pay your debts to the spectators who keep it alive. They don't want to do that here, but that's part of my job."

Gussie's panties would probably look dowdy today. But they were considered revolutionary nearly twenty-five years ago. Some men, it was reported, stretched out on the ground along the walks to the court in order to get a worm's eye view of Moran's bottom. In the early days, showing an ankle on the tennis court was believed risqué. Violet Sutton once told a reporter how uncomfortable it was to play serious tennis at the turn of the century:

"It was a wonder we could move at all," she said. "We wore a long undershirt, pair of drawers, two petticoats, white linen corset cover, duck shirt, shirtwaist, long white silk stockings and a floppy hat. We were soaking wet when we finished a match."

Even in the liberated 1970's, Billie Jean King could still cause titters at Forest Hills by wearing a modestly transparent dress.

Teddy's credo, which was wholeheartedly subscribed to by most of the players, was that as entertainers the women owed it to the public to look attractive. There was nothing wrong either, he felt, with "discreet sex" in the way they dressed on court, provided it also fit his couturier notions of style. Thus the lace panties, a fluffy number of tiered ruffles preferred by such players as Kerry Harris, Patti Hogan and Jeanne Evert, over the more conservative short-shorts that Billie Jean worn under her dresses. Thus, too, the halter-style dress worn by Francoise Durr and the one-bare-shoulder dress created for Kristien Kemmer. Teddy had had to educate the women to dress right, he explained, as well as to devise solutions to such athletic problems as sweat and body distortion.

In the early days of the Slims tour, he recalled, the women thought nothing of coming on court in dirty T-shirts, sloppy shorts, sweaters that looked as if they had been slept in. Even after they had dresses, they soon found that they couldn't take proper care of them because dry-cleaning or professional pressing was hard to arrange on the road. "At Wimbledon '71, I made two marvelous dresses for Judy Dalton, an Australian player. By the time she got to Houston in September, she looked bloody frightening. The dresses had been washed and unironed for six weeks, unpressed, mussed and horrible. I felt so ashamed," Teddy said. From then on, he made all the dresses of acrylic knit, so they could be washed and tumble-dried. He also eliminated the back zipper. "The last thing a woman wants is to have the hardest bit of their dress on the hardest bit of themselves."

Tinling also forced the women to wear brassieres. Tory Fretz laughingly recalled that, being small-breasted, she had never worn a bra before Teddy came along. "He wouldn't do a dress for me until I got one, so the girls took me out and got me this *thing* that pushed me out to *here!*" It was not as backward a step in the history of feminism as it might seem. The dresses merely fit better when the players wore a bra beneath them. Of course, bras could also be the cause of embarrassing pauses in tournament play. Francoise Durr, a well-endowed woman, was playing against Maria Bueno in Australia once when her bra strap suddenly broke. She had to excuse herself, run into the locker room and change. There were still times when Tory, Kristien Kemmer and Rosie Casals, among others, played bra-less, but the vast majority of women were more comfortable with the support. (The bras they wore were of no special "athletic" design. Marilyn Barnett told me she bought Billie Jean's for her in a Los Angeles department store, ten at a time.)

I had a theory about the distinguishing features of tennis players' figures, which I got to try out on Teddy: small breasts and big feet. But he quashed it, singling out Francoise Durr, Ann Jones and Maria Bueno as examples of those who were well-endowed on top, and Rosie and Chris, who were relatively petite at base. The main difference between tennis pros and other women, he said, was the players' big waists.

Months later, I had to get Billie Jean's measurements to compare with Bobby Riggs's for a "tale of the tape" *The New York Times* was publishing as a joke before the Astrodome match. Sure enough, her waist was bigger than it might have been on a similarly built woman—she was 35-27-36½.

Without exception, Tinling continued, the pros were larger on one side of their bodies from shoulder to waist, the result of years of bending, stretching and rotating one

139

arm. Margaret Court was the most distorted: "She had such enormous rotation her shoulder comes right out of her dress." One of Teddy's jobs in designing the women's dresses—and the reason why they needed individual fittings —was camouflaging the distortion.

Tinling, Hambuechen and King were all men betting on the continued growth of the women's professional game. Gene Scott, who was involved in tennis both as a business-man and as a pro, was not. A fair player in his day, Gene, now thirty-five, was a Yale-educated lawyer who did some managing, acted as counsel to the U. S. Open, and competed in the over-thirty-five men's division. When I asked him one day in the tearoom about the drawing power of women's tennis, he brushed it off as the clever but artificial creation of sponsors such as Virginia Slims.

"Look," he said, "Philip Morris undoubtedly got its money's worth out of the promotion—the 'Slims girls' have become like Kleenex, a brand name entering the language. But you've got to have spectators, and spectator-wise, it's not that big a sport. A good high school basketball team draws four thousand people. A Slims or U.S.L.T.A. tourna-ment is lucky to do that. And the reason is women's tennis is like a new rope act come to town. The question is, how long will the novelty last?"

Scott had once played Billie Jean in an exhibition, spotted her 10 points in a 21-point game and had won anyway. Did he or other men players like to watch the women play? Scott subscribed to the separate-and-inferior doctrine.

"I can admire Billie Jean as a super athlete, but it's like watching a boy who's best in his age group. Billie Jean is the best woman, but she still doesn't have the speed, the strength of the men. We all like to watch Billie Jean and Evonne as athletes. But if I want to see sprinters, I prefer to watch the best sprinters in the world."

Scott smiled. "So what I do is watch the pretty ones. I like to watch their legs."

140

It was amusing. The one time I had seen Gene Scott play was when he hit with New York's Mayor John Lindsay at a Central Park exhibition a few years ago. The only thing I remembered about the match was that Lindsay had better legs.

Centre Court

THE QUARTERFINAL ROUND CAME WITHOUT A MAJOR UP-
set. All eight of the women seeds—Court, King, Goolagong,
Evert, Casals, Wade, Melville and Morozova—made it.
Ditto the semifinals, as Margaret beat Morozova, Chris beat
Rosie, Evonne beat Wade, King beat Melville. It was like
watching someone fill out a crossword puzzle in ink. There
were far too few upsets in the women's game for my liking,
I decided. Without upsets the play became predictable.

The day of the semifinals I dropped into a London
bookmaking office to check the odds. (Betting on Wimbledon is a grand and legal sport in England.) The line followed the seedings: Court was 6 to 4 to win the title, Billie
Jean 7 to 4, Goolagong 4 to 1, Evert 8 to 1. Ann Jones, an
astute observer, had told me she would be leaning toward
Evonne, who had been on one of her sizzling streaks all
week. I put £1 on Evonne, mainly because the odds weren't
good enough on King. It was, though I didn't know it then,
the last time I would ever bet against the Old Lady.

The Evert-Court match was the first semifinal on the
bill. The two of them strode out into Centre Court together:
Margaret was pale—she said later she had been suffering
all week from a reaction to some penicillin she had taken to
cure a virus. Chris was stone-faced—she said later she went
out thinking, "The way I've been playing there's no *way* I'm
gonna beat her."

But from the first game, it became apparent that the Ice Dolly was in command. With a quickness that stunned the crowd she picked off the first four games, lobbing faultlessly, passing Margaret consistently when the bigger woman tried to rush the net, winning the set 6-1.

Margaret took the second by the same score, retreating to the baseline. She had won only a battle, though, not the war. Even from a distance I thought I saw The Arm's broad shoulders sag. She double-faulted to lose a crucial game in the third set, and with Chris ahead 5-1, a variation of a recent political campaign slogan popped into my head: "She is fresh and everyone else is tired." Someone in the crowd shouted, "Come on, Margaret!" It was too late. On match point, she netted a backhand and it was all over.

Chris had finally smeared the ink on the crossword puzzle, wiping out Margaret's dream of becoming the first woman to repeat the Grand Slam. But that was not the important thing. Chris had proved herself. Standing at the baseline in a white scoop-neck dress with baby-blue trim, Chris Evert yelped like a puppy, grinned, dashed toward the net . . . and then collected herself, walking the last few steps slowly, head down, as Margaret came forward to shake her hand.

In the locker room, the Ice Dolly stood alone against a wall, expressionless. The door opened. Laurie Fleming, her best friend on the circuit after Jeanne, stepped inside. A glance passed between them. "Oh, Laurie," Chris said, "I was going to cry before, but I wanted to wait for you!" And they both burst into tears.

Billie Jean and Evonne walked onto the court directly after the Evert-Court match was over. The crowd buzzed with a combination of anticipation and fear. If Billie Jean won, she would, first of all, spoil a nice day in the sun for 24,000 spectators who, like the rest of England, adored the ever-smiling Evonne. Second, she would set up the first all-American final since 1957. Third, and worse, it would be a final starring The Woman They Loved to Hate (Billie Jean) and The Girl They Weren't Terribly Fond Of (Chris).

Watching from a secret spot on the photographers' stand beside the Royal Box, which Ed Fernberger had kindly shown me after the British powers-that-be refused me a regular press badge, I couldn't wait for all the Redcoats' fears to be confirmed. Forgetting my £1 on Evonne, I rooted madly for Billie Jean. It was entirely unnecessary; she won in three sets.

The date, fittingly enough, was July 4.

"On ladies' finals day you'll notice the hats," Ann Jones had told me. "It's part of the tradition. The women spectators all dress up and parade in their big hats. We used to hang out of the dressing room and look at them. 'Oooh, have you seen that one,' and 'Doesn't *she* look a sight!' "

The hats were out in force on finals day, as were members of the Royal Family, decorously perched on the edges of their green wicker chairs in the Royal Box directly behind the baseline at Centre Court. It was an imposing place, more like the enclosed lawn of a duke's castle than a sports stadium, its grass, its seats, its wooden awnings all green as the English countryside. Players were awestruck the first time they stepped out onto Centre Court in the same way as opera singers were the first time they took the stage at La Scala. "My first year at Wimbledon," Althea Gibson told me, "I walked out there, I saw all those people looking down on us, and it made me feel quite small. I said to myself, Althea, you're going to watch the ball, not the people. I won the first set 6-0. Then I looked up—and I lost the second set 6-0."

The afternoon was to be a double-bonus for the spectators—women's-singles final and men's-singles final on the same day. The women's match had been postponed when, ten minutes before it was to start the previous day, the rains had come. Chris and Billie Jean had waited for three hours in the locker room before Mike Gibson, the referee, had finally called it off. Billie Jean, surrounded by Rosie Casals, Francoise Durr and other friends, had cracked jokes, gabbed, gossiped. Chris had sat curled up in a ball on a couch. King had been there before: seven Wimbledon finals, four victories. Evert, once again, was the New Girl.

Now, a band played "Moon River" in a corner of the stadium while the crowd waited in the cool, bright sunshine for the two to appear. I still had not done my interview with Billie Jean. It had been scheduled for that morning, but Marilyn Barnett postponed it because of the finals. As a consolation, Marilyn had done me a favor—she had given me a complimentary ticket to the "friends of the players" box in the corner of the stadium just below the press box, where I sat behind Queen King's own royal family: Larry, pale and nervous in a blue blazer; Rosie, snapping pictures with her Pentax; Marilyn; Dick Butera, the president of the Hilton Head Island racquet club that Billie Jean was affiliated with; others. In the corner, in a handsome white hat, black-and-white striped jersey and white pants, sat Colette Evert. As fellow members of the subculture, she and Larry King were occasional tennis partners, part of the group of nonplaying circuit riders organized into what amounted to an informal amateur satellite tournament during various circuit weeks. "Larry," Colette said as she moved toward her seat, "I just hope it's a match."

"I'm more nervous than Billie Jean is," he replied.

Billie Jean looked anything but nervous as she and Chris made their entrance, each carrying a bouquet, Billie Jean's flowers blue and lavender to match the lavender in her sweater, Chris's yellow and red to match the yellow ribbon in her hair. As they warmed up it occurred to me that the British, in their anti-Americanism, were missing what I saw, with hyperbolic enthusiasm, as a classic confrontation. Youth versus Age . . . Ingenue versus Leading Lady . . . Anne Baxter versus Bette Davis . . . Coquette versus Jock . . . Florida versus California . . . Conformist versus Rebel . . . Fair Rosamund versus Eleanor of Aquitaine. . . . I was trying to remember my Euripides when the match began.

The first set was not a battle, it was a lesson in weap-

onry, taught by a scarred Marine with a chestful of medals
to a smart but green recruit. Billie Jean had none of the
grace of Goolagong, nor the majesty of Court, nor the ham-
merlock concentration of Evert. Instead, like Rosie, she
had every shot in the book, and unlike Rosie, she knew
exactly how and when to use them. From the first point,
she carved up Chris's game like a Benihana chef slicing up
meat on a hibachi table. Chop, spin, slice, drive, smash . . .
a devastating flat backhand, a delicate touch vol'ey, a
murderous overhead smash. King's quickness was unbelievable, her placements infallible. I had seen Billie Jean play
many times in past years, and I had always wound up paying more attention to her antics—the muttered curses, the
drop-dead looks at the linesmen, the incessant babbling
("Bi-LEE!" "I can't stand it!" "HIT the ball!"), the arms
flung at the sky—than to her strokes. Here, she kept her
mouth shut, and I saw the athlete behind the entertainer.
She gave Chris nothing good to hit. The ball caromed off
her racquet with a different velocity every time. There was
something more beautiful at work here than Evonne's grace.
It was the joyous attack of a superbly trained Kung Fu
artist, it was Brooks Robinson scooping up a grounder in
the hole and then whipping the ball dead on into the first
baseman's mitt, it was a shit-kicking guitar riff by Jimi
Hendrix. It was the loveliest, meanest set of tennis I'd ever
seen.

In the sixth game, Billie Jean, serving for the set, at
40-15, smashed an overhead at the net that caught Chris
going the wrong way. The muscles in her tanned right arm
rippling, Billie Jean heaved the ball she was holding over
the net, and with it, a glowering look. The look said: "Not
this time, kid." It was 6-0. Chris had won exactly nine
points.

When Billie Jean broke Chris's serve in the first game
of the second set, I leaned forward. "Is this what the
English call a drubbing?" I asked Larry. He shook his
head. "It's not over yet. I've seen Billie win the first set 6-1,
be up 5-1 in the second, and lose. The only time I relax

is when she's ahead two sets to love." I glanced at Colette, wanting to say something comforting, but nothing came to mind. Larry looked back and asked her if she had any gum. She wordlessly passed him a stick of Doublemint.

Chris got some sting back in her strokes as the set progressed, picking up nine straight points to make it 4-3 in her favor. The set grew tighter, with Chris pulling ahead 5-4. As they changed sides, Billie Jean glanced up at our box. Larry held up a fist.

Billie Jean held service for 5-5, broke Chris for 6-5 as the younger girl's lobs began to go astray, and closed it out in the next game. The exhibition had lasted little more than an hour. The groundskeepers rolled out a green carpet for a member of the Royal Family, who presented Billie Jean the shiny gold plate. The champ once more, Billie Jean held it high over her head in both hands, displaying it to the crowd with relish. The applause began reluctantly, then swelled. She looked as if she would have liked to stick out her tongue.

Billie Jean came into the windowless interview room a half hour later, teacup in hand, and the reporters applauded too. She was brimming with cheerfulness, a proud veteran who still had a lot of kid in her herself. "Guess what? I've been off ice cream since February. I'm so excited —I can have some now." She licked her lips and grinned the big, toothy California smile. She called the first set the best she'd ever played in a big tournament. She babbled about the weather, the wind, her overhead. ("It was really *shaaaky,*" she said, singing the last word.) For a moment, she became serious as a newsman asked if she derived special satisfaction from the day's win. "I lost to Chris Evert love and one in Fort Lauderdale a while back," she replied crisply. "And I guess I've never forgotten it."

Billie Jean slumped into a flowered wicker chaise longue in the deserted locker room, the last player left at Wimbledon.

It was the day after her singles victory, and minutes earlier, she had curtsied toward the Royal Box for the third time in the tournament.

Rosie Casals had once said, "Wimbledon is the Old Lady's house," and during this 1973 fortnight, she had outdone herself asserting her ownership. She had put on an unbelievable show of championship, clutch match play. In two days, she had played six matches, 139 pressure-packed games in Centre Court, and had walked off with everything but the crown jewels. She had won her second Wimbledon triple—singles, doubles (with Rosie) and mixed doubles (with Owen Davidson).

Now, alone in the spacious upstairs dressing area (there were actually three separate women's locker rooms) except for the attendant and me, still waiting for my interview, she was, as she put it bluntly, wiped out.

The attendant, an elderly lady, picked up the last of the towels lying around. "Well, we do hope to see you again next year," she said. "Oh, don't worry," Billie Jean replied, slipping into a pair of white clogs, "I'll be back."

Marilyn walked in with a worried look. "Billie Jean, the car's downstairs but you're gonna have to make a run for it. There are hundreds of people down there waiting for you," she exclaimed.

A blissful smile spread across Billie Jean's face. She jumped up, the adrenalin almost visibly flowing through her body. "Isn't it wonderful?" she bubbled. "Can't last forever, you know."

With that, she swept out of the locker room, down the stairs. As they caught sight of her, the fans broke into sustained cheers, and she waded in, the smile never leaving her face. Programs, hats, racquet covers, ice cream wrappers—she signed everything thrust at her. Someone plunked a baby in her arms; she held it up as she had the trophy the day before, kissed it for a photographer, handed it back. Finally, after ten minutes, two bobbies materialized by her side and propelled her into the back seat of the car.

It was an exit worthy of the Beatles. With hordes of

young boys and girls dashing after the car, we drove through the gate, Marilyn insisting that Billie Jean lie flat on the back seat so we could drive up the road a bit and then double back. She giggled like an insane eleven-year-old as she stretched out.

"Oh man," shrieked the world champion of women's tennis, looking up through the sun roof, "what a great view of the trees!"

The Old Lady

SITTING UNDER A BIG SHADE TREE BY THE BANKS OF THE
Thames, we discussed tennis and the women's movement.
Marilyn had doubled back over Church Road outside
the All-England Club to the Lakeside Tennis Club directly
across the street, where she had led us to a grassy embankment overlooking the river, its quiet broken only by the
occasional quack of a duck.

"Ooooooh, my whole body is so tired," Billie Jean
said, stretching out her aching legs on some pages of the
International *Herald Tribune* that Marilyn had laid down.
But as she began to talk, the tiredness melted away, and,
still "psyched up" from her victories, she bubbled like a per-
colator, talking the way she played—fast, instinctively, the
words running together, the ideas bouncing scatter-shot
from one subject to the next, her light-blue eyes staring
with a near-hypnotic urgency. She was, I discovered, at
her best after a big win. Listening to her, I felt as if I were
watching a manic Aimee Semple MacPherson on an am-
phetamine high. Winning, for Billie Jean, was a more potent
drug than any chemist could devise, a more inspirational
gospel than any scripture could preach. "Sometimes," Julie
Anthony told me, "it takes so much togetherness when
you're on the court that afterwards all the glue seems to
come apart in some people. I have heard Billie Jean at times
just absolutely babble incoherently."

She was at that stage now, but it was not incoherent, simply disjointed. And when I was able to put the pieces together, she made marvelous sense. With major exceptions like Heldman, Anthony, and Casals, too many of the players had disappointed me with their lack of understanding of the relationship between their role and the women's movement. They were jocks. Their minds did not think about those things—they let their bodies do the talking for them. Billie Jean once said herself that the words *masculine* and *feminine* should be deleted from the language because "all women tennis players are jocks." Nevertheless, she above all the others understood perfectly what the movement-tennis relationship was all about. She was a jock who had spent her career discovering that she was a pioneer, that no one was yet ready to delete the terms for gender from the sports vocabulary, that women would still be second-class sports champions until they fought for the right to be classed in the same league as a Joe Namath or a Wilt Chamberlain. In a sense, feminism had been forced on her; she used it as a tool to win the superstar acceptance she craved. Billie Jean liked seeing her face on the cover of *Ms.,* but she loved seeing it on the cover of *Sports Illustrated* even more.

At her final Wimbledon press conference, a woman had asked what she thought of being listed as "Mrs. L. W. King." "I think," she had replied, "that feminists get hung up on too many trivial things."

Now, I asked whether she didn't see that apparently trivial listing as indicative of a whole set of unliberated attitudes that prevailed in the game. "Yes," she agreed, "it's indicative. But that's still not of particular importance. We can't just talk about those things, we've got to go out there and *change* things. I'm interested in the women's movement, but from an action point of view, not an intellectual one. Tennis helps the women's movement just by *doing*. We're *there,* we're visual, like blacks in sports who helped their movement. If people see us out there every day, that changes people's minds, not *talking* about it." Billie Jean's feminist vision, however, was still not wide enough to appreciate the contradiction in the hiring of a man to administer her Women's Tennis Association.

The consummate female jock, King had picked up feminism the way she had picked up tennis as a child; she fiddled around with the basic equipment, juggled the pieces impatiently until they worked for her, then played to the hilt to win. The realization of what feminism meant dawned on her only as the movement became articulate in the 1960's, but for Billie Jean, as for so many women in other male-dominated professions, it had been a case of putting a label on much of what her life had stood for all along.

The only thing she had ever wanted to be was a champion. "I've talked to a lot of champions, and the one thing we all have is a certain sameness of motivation," she said. "Pressure—I love it. I don't know why. Why do you rise to an occasion? Pressure. It spurs you on. I feel the adrenalin flowing. And champions never look back, like, I think back only if I think that it can help me *today*."

She thought back, for a moment. "All I know is that as an eleven-year-old child I used to dream about being a great tennis player. Numero Uno! Wow!" She let out a whoop, like an eleven-year-old child, and, as if I were watching a movie, my mind did a slow dissolve. . . .

Eleven-year-old Billie Jean Moffitt, pudgy, near-sighted, fireman's daughter, on a softball sandlot in Long Beach, crouching into the ready position at shortstop. She was a star infielder on the firemen's softball team, star forward on the girls' basketball team. "My mother"—she chuckled—"was always saying, 'Be a lady.' What does that mean? I loved to get out there and run around, and if you really love something that way, nothing's gonna stop you."

Nothing did. She asked her father to suggest a sport more ladylike. (She was kicked off the basketball team, her father told me, because she refused to play by the zone rules of the women's game, insisting instead on driving right through the zones for the basket.) Her father suggested tennis. "What's tennis?" she asked.

152

In the public parks, she found out, insisting on developing a style of play as aggressive as her style had been in basketball. Coaches wanted her to lay back at the baseline and practice ground strokes. Billie Jean kept charging the net, asking, "What's that shot where you hit the ball before it bounces?"

At twelve she won her first tournament. Her parents struggled to pay for her new enthusiasm; she went through a pair of sneakers a week. At fifteen, when she first came east for a tournament, a coach, Frank Brennan, suggested she switch from nylon to gut strings. Billie Jean said she couldn't afford gut. "I'll buy you all the gut you need," said Frank Brennan. At sixteen, unknown, she knocked Margaret Smith (later Court) out of the Wimbledon singles in the first round, to the astonishment of a tennis press that had already chosen Margaret heiress to the throne once held by Lenglen and Wills. At seventeen, she won her first Wimbledon doubles title, at twenty-two, her first singles. Still pudgy, her eyes framed by harlequin glasses, her hair cropped short and boyish, Billie Jean was Numero Uno.

"And nobody," she was saying as my imaginary movie slow-dissolved back to the present, "gave a shit."

Rod Laver and Arthur Ashe got the headlines when they won national championships; Billie Jean got the last paragraph of the story. Writers asked Laver and Ashe about their plans for the upcoming tournaments; they asked Billie Jean when she and her husband were going to settle down and have children. Ashe called for black pride and was applauded; Billie Jean signed a petition for legal abortion and was condemned. "We've got to get women's tennis off the women's pages and into the sports pages," she once snapped at a women's page reporter, and I suspected that she remained ambivalent about female reporters because she equated them with second-class coverage.

What feminism meant to Billie Jean was making bigger headlines on the sports pages than the Lavers and the Namaths. It meant that gradually, as the movement took hold in the late 1960's and early 1970's, women tennis players were becoming accepted as athletes, not as freaks, as role models rather than as tomboys in a state of arrested development, as careerists rather than as amateurs waiting to catch a husband.

"Tennis has always been more accepted for women than team sports," she explained, now looking out over the river. "Probably because it was more ladylike, because it's not a contact sport. But people are starting to look up to us now. We've made it okay for a girl to say, 'If I enjoy playing tennis and sweating, I don't care what my boyfriend thinks.' Now a lot of people are thinking women tennis players are great *because* we're athletes—blood 'n' guts—because, if a woman's been able to get to the top in sports she's got to have something special."

The reason more women had not gone into sports in the first place was twofold, she continued. As a youngster in junior high school and even college (she attended Cal State at Los Angeles for two years), she recalled, "the budget was nil" for girls' sports. The opportunities were not there because the acceptance was not there. "It wasn't the thing to do—be an athlete. A girl isn't really accepted by her peer group or society. If a man's an athlete, he's looked up to, business doors open up. Women are just getting into that now."

It was Billie Jean, always Billie Jean, who had forced the issue, hammered it home to the tennis establishment and her reluctant fellow travelers in the women's game alike. "Three years ago, you wouldn't believe the trouble we had organizing the Slims, getting sixteen girls to join us. Too many of them were still, are still, hung up on outside gratification. They were afraid to take the risk. They were going through the same things I did—the conflict about making a stink, committing themselves to stop worrying about whether it was ladylike to make tennis a profession. I didn't want them to go through the same thing! That was the point! For three years I argued for a women's players association because that was the only way we'd get tennis out of the hands of the associations and into our own. The idea of controlling their own destiny threw them for a loop! For me it was the most natural thing in the world. If they're becoming more professional now, it's because a couple of us are pushing."

There were some players who thought Billie Jean pushed too far, some who felt that her drive to organize the women's tour and the players association was part of a King power grab. "Whatever Billie Jean says she's doing for *us,* she's really only doing it for herself," contended one foreign player. It was difficult to understand their anger. Even if what they said was true, Billie Jean's efforts had still put more prize money in their pockets than many of them had ever hoped to win. But revolutionaries were never universally loved, charismatic leaders never immune to envy, especially when, as in Billie Jean's case, they were supreme egotists who could get nasty and impatient with those who did not unquestionably march to their drummer. The women's movement itself was no exception to the pattern, nor was the women's tennis movement.

Besides, in addition to everything else, the other women had to face Billie Jean across the net every so often. There, despite her repeated insistence that "I won't be around forever, someone else will take my place, we've got to develop ten, twenty new stars," she had the annoying habit of beating the pants off almost every one of them. Later in the year, at a press conference with fifteen-year-old Robin Tenney, Billie Jean went into a long inspirational rap about the marvelous future open to the Robin Tenneys of the world . . . not before the match, but after she had beaten Robin 6-1, 6-1. Still another time, she mentioned that the great former star Alice Marble had once told her she'd never be a champion. "It kind of stunned her to see somebody want it the way she wanted it," Billie Jean said. "Some champions don't really want anyone ever to take their place. I think that hurts sports. I know how I felt at fifteen and sixteen. I wanted it so badly! Now, I *like* to see the kids at fifteen and sixteen want it just as badly."

Of course, if they really wanted it, they'd have to drag

a kicking and screaming King off the throne first. It wasn't hypocrisy—Billie Jean quite simply considered losing to be the Original Sin. Nevertheless, being the kind of Numero Uno she was did not simplify dealings on the organizational front.

    With Marilyn sitting cross-legged and mum beside us like a frail paisley Buddha, Billie Jean hopscotched from the women's movement to golf, from sports aesthetics to injuries. I had never had a better interview—she did all the work for me. I had never met anyone with such a relentlessly positive attitude on every subject; it was as if she had memorized every Norman Vincent Peale sermon.

    When I asked what other sports she played nowadays, she told how she had taken up golf under the tutelage of Jane Blalock, the controversial pro golfer. "I drove them crazy!" she shrieked. "I was running from tee to tee, put my tee in, hit the ball, then run down the fairway! They told me, 'That's not the way we do it.' And I said, 'Well, that's the way I'm doing it!' " She threw her head back with a great big "Hah!" and concluded the story with her plans for a joint pro tennis and golf tournament at Hilton Head Island, her talks with Blalock about bringing women from the two fields together for pro-am exhibitions, and her reason for rarely playing catch any more with her brother, Randy Moffitt, a pitcher with the San Francisco Giants. ("I'd have to duck!") Most of the women I had spoken to liked other sports: Val Ziegenfuss played golf and often wound up in a family volleyball game when she visited her parents (her father was once basketball coach of the University of San Diego); Lesley Hunt was an avid surfer; Julie Anthony loved to ski. But who else could organize a women's sports federation while dashing around the fairway?

    I asked about superstitions. In a completely unscientific survey during the season, I found that roughly half the women had definite superstitions they would talk about— a lucky dress, a necklace, a pair of shoes. Julie Heldman claimed that as a youngster she had been so fanatic about letting the ball bounce twice to her from a ball boy when it was her serve that if it only bounced once, she would let it go by. Betty Stove was careful not to step on the alley lines coming off the court to change sides. Kris Kemmer got feelings about individual balls and would insist on serving with one until she lost a point. Margaret Court insisted she had no superstitions, but when a museum in San Diego asked if it might have the dress that she had worn losing to Bobby Riggs, she gladly donated it because she had no intention of ever wearing it again.

From Billie Jean, naturally, I got, not an answer on superstitions, but a dissertation. "Well, there's my bathtub," she began. "I always take a bath in the same bathtub each year at Wimbledon. That's *my* bathtub. And I like my jewelry . . . don't feel on balance without it." She held up her left wrist, on which she wore three gold bracelets: a plain circle, which she had had since she was sixteen; a link chain, which was Swedish; and a solid one with a design on it that had been a gift. Finally, there were the dresses. "I get flashes, see? Like the lavender one with the initials I wore yesterday, in the finals? I told Teddy last year that was *the* dress."

At her last press conference, someone had asked Billie Jean, "What makes you you?" Pressure, she had replied. I wondered how hard it was, after almost nineteen years as a competitor, to get "up" for each match. Was it just as easy to win Wimbledon the fifth time as the first? Was it just as much of a kick to win $100,000 for a third year as it was for the first?

The words came gushing out, a fire hydrant suddenly uncapped: how she had almost quit at the beginning of 1972 because she had another injury (she pulled a stomach muscle playing catch one day with ball boys), how it grew tougher and tougher to get "psyched" for an ordinary match, how she wanted to go on to other things. "But then I said to myself, 'Oh, Billie, you can't live on your past laurels.'" Instead, she sat down and wrote out her objectives for the year—another winning Virginia Slims circuit, another

$100,000, another Wimbledon victory, the Women's Tennis Association. (She claimed she had never written down goals before, but Ziegenfuss told me that one previous year she had asked the other women for suggestions. Why not shoot for an unbeaten match play record for the year? they said. All right, she said . . . and went on to win every match but three.)

"I got double pleasure out of Wimbledon this year because we formed the Players Association too," she remarked. "You know, the older you get, the more you find out about yourself. I've *got* to have goals to keep going, and I've found my interests getting wider. I've got all kinds of plans—for team tennis, for the Association, I want to get into more businesses." She was starting a women's sports magazine, she was going to be a team tennis coach (the first woman coach of an intersex squad), she would (though she did not say it just then, because it had not yet been publicly announced) play Bobby Riggs for $100,000. Her energy astounded me. Linda Tuero, a relatively minor player, only twenty-one years old, who had won nothing higher than the Italian Championship, had remarked with some asperity that she didn't think she could ever be Number 1 because "I just don't want to spend twenty-four hours a day on tennis; I may be a professional but I'm also a woman, and I want to be a woman first." Yet here was a woman eight years her senior, who had collected more wins than Tuero had played matches, who could devote twenty-four hours a day to tennis and a dozen other pursuits, who thus, by being a complete person, made Tuero look like a pouty adolescent, and who had a sense of humor to boot.

It was getting late, and a small group of boys had discovered our hiding place. As we got set to leave, I asked Billie Jean whether she got sheer physical pleasure out of hitting tennis balls after nineteen years. "It's music, it's dancing, sometimes I sing to myself to get a rhythm," she bubbled. "To hit a ball right, when you're on the balls of your feet, your body's working the way you want it, it's the greatest thing in the whole wide world!"

"Does anything else give you that much pleasure?" I asked. She grinned from one gold earring to the other.

"Sex!" she shrieked. "Don't print that!"

The half-dozen cockney boys who had gathered with their bicycles at the top of the embankment followed us to the car, pouncing on King for autographs. One boy frantically emptied a cigarette pack to get a scrap of paper. Billie Jean patiently signed each one. As she pulled the car out of the club, she watched them trailing us on their bikes and said seriously, "You know, those are the kind of kids who never get to *see* Wimbledon, except on television."

She took one last look at the gates of the All-England Club ("Good-bye, Wimbledon," she sang out the window) and headed toward London. Her triple win had been only the first of her performances that day. The interview had been the second, and she deserved an Oscar for the third, the drive home. She maneuvered a car the way she played tennis, too—one hand expertly directing the wheel, the other fiddling with the radio, the mouth chattering a running commentary on everything under the sun. "Wouldya lookit that guy *strut* on the sidewalk over there. . . . Right on! The British must have had an awful time with Chris and me yesterday—two Yankees! Hah! Boy, they really hate us. They think it's still World War Two or something, they think they're still Numero Uno. They're so hung up on rules they're inefficient—you can't go here, you can't do this . . . if they spent half as much time on scheduling the matches right as they did on rules, I wouldn't have had to play six in two days. . . . Margaret? They'll be talking forever about what a great champ Margaret is because she *looks* that way—long legs. . . . Well, she doesn't have good hands, and it's not how long your legs are anyway, or what kind of a body you have, it's what you do with it, baby, it's how you play the crucial points. . . . Lookit that lorry! . . ."

By the time we reached the Gloucester, she had replayed the Battle of Britain, cursed out three slow drivers, and had given me careful instructions on whom to interview for my book. "Oh, the old letdown's coming," she told Marilyn, with a yawn, as she pulled into the driveway. "I'm gonna sleep twenty hours a day for six days. Zonkereno!"

Two days later, in New York, I was still exhausted from Wimbledon plus jet lag, while Billie Jean was bounding all over the Town Tennis Club for two hours at the press conference announcing the Riggs match.

Right on, Numero Uno, and Zonkereno to you, too.

Allaire

Madame Superstar

BILLIE JEAN, PALE AND GRIM-FACED, STRADDLED A BENCH in the locker room of the Allaire Racquet Club and played with a bottle of Bubble-Up. "I'm sick of not having any privacy," she muttered. "I just wish people would stop touching me. People keep coming up and touching me, having to talk. Maybe I should hire a couple of bodyguards. Yeah, it's great that people are really interested in the match. I guess I can't have everything." She took another slug from the bottle.

"It's just that everybody's pulling from all sides. Everybody wants a *piece* of me!"

A month had passed since her Wimbledon triumphs, and the manic eleven-year-old had metamorphosed into a harried Madame Superstar, as Teddy Tinling aptly named her. The catalyst was a gentleman named Bobby Riggs.

Three days after winning the triple at Wimbledon, Billie Jean had signed up for the Riggs match, throwing down the gauntlet of feminism at a New York press conference that had more in common with "All in the Family" than with tennis. (Bobby: "I won Wimbledon in '39." Billie: "Sorry I missed it—I wasn't born yet." Bobby: "I've been taking 415 vitamin pills a day." Billie: "He'd better start taking twice as many, and throw in some Geritol too.") The drumbeat of publicity had not stopped since.

Every place she went, Billie Jean was besieged with

questions about the Riggs match, set for September 20 in the Astrodome. Las Vegas made book on it, fans spent cocktail parties arguing it, *Time* and *Newsweek* planned cover stories on it. Johnny Carson wanted her to talk, Sunbeam wanted her to use its hairsetting mist, *The Wall Street Journal* wanted to do a story on her finances. With Hank Aaron, Secretariat and Bobby Riggs, Billie Jean King was suddenly catapulted into the national sweepstakes for biggest sports story of the year.

Billie Jean had been waiting all her life for this. She had lobbied for her name in lights, courted the mass media hype, demanded the public's attention. Now she *had* it, and she was beginning to discover that being a Superstar was a twenty-five-hour-a-day job. The pressure—a very different kind from the pressure she knew how to cope with on a tennis court—was taking its toll.

For one thing, the business of playing tennis had started to get in her way. The Virginia Slims circuit had resumed in August (as had the U.S.L.T.A. circuit). Billie Jean, committed to play each of the five Slims events plus Forest Hills while preparing for the Riggs match, had won the first summer tournament in Denver, then had reached the finals against Court in Nashville, the second stop. The Nashville match had nearly been postponed a day because of rain. When Billie Jean learned of the possible rescheduling, she threw a fit, threatening to default; she was due in Los Angeles the next morning to film a $50,000-plus Sunbeam commercial. The final was eventually played late in the afternoon. As soon as she dropped the third set, King had stormed off the court and rushed to the airport without waiting for the post-game ceremonies in which she was to be presented with the runner-up check. "What are we supposed to do," asked one of the sponsors, "slip the check under her bathroom door while she's showering?"

Now, having just flown back east to the New Jersey shore for the third Slims summer tournament, after a twenty-four-hour trip to California for the commercial, Billie Jean drummed her fingers impatiently on the bench when I asked whether she might be overcommitting herself. "I've got tennis and I've got commercials to do and they're equally important. Sunbeam could have sued me. I only have one day off. It's my *business,* y'know," she snapped.

The business of the moment was the Jersey Shore Tennis Classic, and it was hers, all hers. The tournament was being played at a brand-new private tennis club owned by a local dentist and several friends who had signed up the Slims tour thinking it would be a good promotion. With Billie Jean playing, they hoped to break even on gate receipts. Her name and face were everywhere—on a huge sign hung outside the entrance to the club, on the sides of "official tournament cars" borrowed from members to transport players around, on a T-shirt sold in the club's pro shop.

The club was located in the middle of the New Jersey summer resort strip along the ocean not far from Atlantic City. The strip was lined with decaying white elephant hotels whose patrons were as cracked and decrepit as their rooms. Some of the stars had been booked into one of the largest of these hotels; the average age of the inhabitants seemed to be eighty-seven. Marilyn Barnett took one look at the unair-conditioned $60-a-day "suite" that had been reserved for Billie Jean and herself and immediately picked up the phone book to search for a Holiday Inn. (She couldn't find one.) Rosie Casals later recalled listening to two women in rocking chairs on the hotel's front porch discuss the dangers of having a stroke by staying out in the sun too long. "Unfortunately," Rosie said, "it rained that day."

Fortunately for the Jersey Shore Classic, the tournament was played on the club's six indoor courts (there were also four outdoor ones), because it rained almost every day. The players, almost all of whom were staying, as usual, with local families, had hoped to get some serious sunbathing done. Instead, they wound up hanging around the club, sitting in the big leather armchairs in the lounge writing letters, reading *I'm OK, You're OK,* playing backgammon, watching the matches, and gossiping. In a corner of the lounge near a large fireplace, Peachy Kellmeyer, the tour director, had put up a bulletin board with sheets listing practice times as well as the week's optional leisure-time activities—a visit to the local racetrack, a sailing expedition, a Johnny Cash concert at a nearby fairground. The players who signed up for the activities were almost all qualifiers who expected to be knocked out of the tournament early.

Backgammon had nearly replaced Scrabble this year as a favorite players' pastime. Betty Stove, the big Dutch player who spoke six languages, had been among the more fanatic Scrabblists. With her doubles partner, Francoise Durr, she often played bilingual games, the two of them keeping a French-English dictionary handy. One time someone had noticed an apparently English word on the board that made no sense. "Well, it looks all right to us," said Betty, shrugging her shoulders.

The players could see matches on three of the courts through a huge glass window that separated the lounge from one side of the playing area. The building had been constructed with a center corridor separating glass-enclosed sets of three courts on either side. Bleachers had been installed on either side of the middle court in one section, making that the main "center court." But for matches played on the courts in the other section, spectators had to stand behind the glass windows in the corridor, watching the players' movements yet hearing none of the sounds. It was like watching a television show from a sealed-off control room. A few of the less experienced players liked the bell-jar aura of the three secondary courts, but the better ones complained that it was eerie, not having a crowd around them.

Gossiping, which ranked with letter-writing as perhaps the most popular pastime, took place at courtside watching other players' matches as well as in the lounge and the locker room. Much of the gossip was tennis insiders' talk—who was signing with World Team Tennis, who beat whom on the U.S.L.T.A. tour, whether or not Ilie Nastase, the mercurial Rumanian male pro star, would pay his misconduct fines. The women took a professional interest in the activities of the men's tennis circuit and many of them counted men players among their friends. They were not sorry, however, that the men played on a separate tour, because they liked having the publicity all to themselves in each town.

Some of the gossip was girl talk, the kind you might hear in a sorority house. A few players were known as big marijuana smokers, and the others would giggle about how someone's hotel room was always reeking of the fumes. (The general consensus among those who indulged was that grass was far better than liquor as a relaxer, because there were no aftereffects. "I'd rather get high on a couple of hits than get high on five drinks and be out of it the next day," one player explained. "I don't really enjoy not having control of my body.")

Men were also a topic of conversation, but as Billie Jean told me, it was usually limited to generalities. "It's really funny," she remarked. "They may say they really like someone as a person, but they don't go into 'Oh, I scored last night.' We've heard the guys talk—like in Sweden once, we were in a sauna bath on the other side of a partition from theirs, they didn't know we were there, and we heard some beautiful things! But it has to do with the way we're brought up. Like a guy is supposed to brag about his conquests, but with women, it's a personal thing, and they may tell their best friend, and that's it. We don't get into any of the real nitty-gritty." She *did* add that the women weren't above taking polls on their male equivalents: "Who we think is the best looking, who's got the best ass, things like that." Nastase and Roger Taylor, the British player, scored high in both departments, she noted.

Whether Billie Jean knew it or not, she and Margaret Court were prime subjects of gossip in New Jersey, for different reasons. There was bitching about King's new star complex, about the fact that she had corraled them into the player's union and then announced that Marilyn would have to sit in as her surrogate on upcoming meetings because Billie Jean was too busy, about how distant she had become in recent weeks, about her relationship with Marilyn and her disinclination to spend time with her husband.

About Margaret, on the other hand, there was disgust at the way she had lost to Bobby Riggs, and suggestions that she had not been at the top of her form after it. In a first-round match at Allaire, she played Mona Shallau, nicknamed the Marengo Kid because her hometown was Marengo, Iowa. A wiry, thoughtful girl who was slowly fighting her way up the prize-money list, Mona stormed ahead of Court 5-2 in the first set. As Margaret walked slowly to the umpire's chair for a changeover, one player in the front row hissed, "What if we whispered very loudly, 'Gee, she hasn't been the same since the Riggs thing.'" There was a chorus of catty chuckles from her colleagues. (Margaret won the match, nevertheless, whizzing through the third set 6-0. When Rosie heard the score later in the evening, she smiled. "Maggie's too cool. She had tickets tonight to Johnny Cash, so she couldn't waste too much time beating Mona. She almost ran me over getting out of the parking lot.")

Billie Jean was not catty about Margaret's loss to Riggs, she was contemptuous. "Margaret played like a donkey," she said, in the haughty tone Maria Callas might have used to describe another diva's rendition of *Norma*.

Billie Jean had been in Honolulu on her way home from a tour of Japan when the massacre took place. "When I finally saw the film of the match and watched him present her with those roses and Margaret curtsy, I yelled 'Margaret, you idiot, you played right into his hands!'" Billie Jean liked to tell people she was forced to play Riggs to avenge Margaret's defeat, for the honor of women's tennis, but that seemed to me only a small part of the explanation for her contempt. After all, Court's loss was responsible in a major way for the fat $100,000 Billie Jean now had a chance to collect if she beat Margaret's conqueror. In reality, Margaret had succumbed to "El Choko," the deadliest sin in the King canon, and for that Billie Jean could not absolve her.

Even if Billie Jean had let Margaret forget about Bobby Riggs, the press would not. As the months had passed, it had become almost ghoulish, the incessant questions, Margaret's pained, careful replies, like a successful surgeon forced to dwell on the one famous patient he had lost. ("Tell us, Margaret, when did you know it was all over? . . .") Court, ever the lady, bore up as best she could under the barrage. "I guess you could say," she mused quietly one afternoon at Allaire, "that I blew the match. It was one of those days." Ever the lady, she put on a show of graciousness toward King. "I didn't know what to expect. Now Billie Jean knows, so I guess the pressure will be a little less on her."

But the pressure was a lot more on Billie Jean, as Margaret must have known. Billie Jean, never the lady, showed it the minute she walked out onto the main court in Allaire to play her first match of the tournament. Francoise Durr, a veteran like King, was her opponent, but her charming Gallic groans and "Ooofs!" on bad calls were no match for Billie Jean's vast repertoire of expressions. On the first line call she didn't like, King merely glared at the linesman, then at the crowd. On the second, she tapped her foot, hands on hips, and looked imploringly at the ceiling. On the third, she glanced at the front stalls and declaimed, "This is supposed to be *professional* tennis." It was a vintage performance, yet disturbing. The joy in her playing seemed gone. After she won, a crowd of children stampeded onto the court around her, but she signed only a few autographs before pushing her way tiredly through the bodies to the locker room.

The next afternoon, the word suddenly flashed through the lounge: Billie Jean had withdrawn from the tournament. In a hastily called press conference, she insisted she had never felt better until, playing a two-on-one practice session, she had slipped on a piece of carpet alongside the court while running wide for a ball, and had strained her weak right knee. "It's not really that bad," she said, tapping the knee through a pair of maroon slacks. But there was a haunted look in her eyes as she added, "I know how it is with injuries. You think you can keep on playing, and you wind up out for weeks instead of days."

I asked where she was going from here. "Crazy," she replied with a weary, mirthless smile. "Wanna come?"

Supporting Cast

DR. HERBERT GRAMBOW, THE CLUB'S PART-OWNER AND tournament director, wandered around the lounge shell-shocked. "The bottom sort of fell out, didn't it?" he said wanly.

Not only had King defaulted on the second day, so had Kerry Melville, the Number 4 seed, with a severe charley horse in her thigh. The news had not only stunned the tournament officials, but had angered some of the ticket holders, who had paid a healthy $265 for a six-seat box for the week. Steve Lurie, a Virginia Slims public relations man, tried to pacify the press corps. "We were thinking of telling everyone Kerry and Billie had been killed in an auto accident, so when you found out it was only knees you'd be so relieved you wouldn't get mad," he said. Nobody thought it was funny.

Dr. Grambow, his face almost the color of his green blazer, slowly crossed off the two names on the big draw chart. The withdrawals had left him with two less-than-spectacular quarterfinal matches that night: Joy Schwikert, a nineteen-year-old qualifier who was to have played King, against Lesley Hunt, and Tory Fretz, who was to have played Melville, against Karen Krantzcke. "Household names—in the Fretz and Schwikert households," cracked New York *News* reporter Dave Hirshey.

Not quite everyone was downcast, however. "Mommy,

Mommy!" Joy Schwikert screamed over the telephone. "I'm in the quarters!"

Tory sat on the couch, hugging herself. "Wow, kid," she whispered with controlled excitement. "900 bucks!" (By reaching the quarters, she had automatically won $900, and would win more if she beat Krantzcke to get into the semifinals.) She marched around the lounge hugging her friends. "Listen, if I win tonight, I'm taking you guys out on the *town*. Champagne, the whole works!" she told them.

Val Ziegenfuss looked as if she could use a night on the town, some champagne, some male companionship, or maybe just a few good wins. Val was one of a clump of middle-range players just below the top level, the kind of player who seemed to have all the strokes but not the mental toughness to climb those few extra steps up the competitive ladder. Like Wendy Overton (who was not in the Allaire tournament because of a bad ankle), Val was among the crop of attractive, aggressive young pros strong enough to make the seedings in a tournament like Allaire but not a major event like Wimbledon, bright enough to line up outside endorsements (in her case, a teaching pro job for a California condominium complex) but nearly unknown to the mass tennis audience, tenacious enough to pull down more than $22,000 in prize money over the year but not to pull off a single stunning upset.

At the ripe old age of twenty-three, she looked over her shoulder and watched the likes of nineteen-year-old Janet Newberry and twenty-one-year-old Kristien Kemmer and fifteen-year-old Jeanne Evert closing in behind her, nudging her aside, moving up on a fast track that didn't allow for slumps or depressions. Valerie, a 5-foot-8-inch Californian with the *zaftig* good looks of a European ski instructress, was paying the price for what she called the "unbelievable competition" the growth of women's tennis had created. She was an athlete, the daughter of an athlete, the girlfriend of an athlete, and she was galloping along with the rest of the pack, struggling to keep pace.

Here, she had been outdistanced in the round of sixteen by Kerry Harris in a grueling, three-set match. She was in a slump. She did not articulate it terribly well, but I thought I could see the strain in her game and in her face.

"For the last eight months I've been fighting myself," she said one day in the Allaire locker room. "I haven't been aggressive enough. It's all an attitude, it's all a matter of desire. You've got to be so determined that nothing else matters. It's waking up and having one purpose in mind. It's being single-minded."

Val had been single-minded most of her life, from the time she grew up, a San Diego tomboy, encouraged in tennis by her father, the basketball coach for the university there.

She had been touring since she was in the juniors, played most of the year, found vacations something of a bore. After Wimbledon, she had come home to San Diego for a three-week rest before the Slims circuit got started again. She had nothing to do. "The days were kind of long, you know? There aren't that many friends at home now after being away for six years. I wound up playing tennis every day."

At Wimbledon, at least, though she had been knocked out of the tournament early, there had been compensations for the lonely grind of the women's tour: men. Val's boyfriend, Dick Dell, was a tennis pro, too, and he had been in England with her. She laughed when I asked if sex was good for her tennis. "I don't know if it helps or hinders," she said candidly. "By the end of the week, physically, after being on the go so much. . . . You're going to the movies, you're going for walks, you go to bed at night and you have some sex, I mean, you get tired! You've still got to put in your hours on the court. On the girls' circuit I'd just come home and go to bed at ten o'clock."

For the single women sex, men, loneliness and competitiveness were all bound up in an intricate web of feelings. The women by and large preferred having their circuit separate from the men's, well aware that they played second fiddle to the men pros whenever the two groups met, as at Wimbledon and Forest Hills. At the same time, it wasn't easy meeting men on the road. Val claimed she could not relate to nonathletes: "Someone who can't throw a football is just such a bore," she said, shrugging. Patti Hogan summed up the problem by saying, "The local talent isn't all that interesting." Women pros didn't yet have groupies the way men tennis players and other athletes did ("Shoot, man, I hope I'm around when that happens," Val said with a grin) and the result was that for too much of the time, the girls slept alone. "It's not as much fun when we're all by ourselves," Val admitted. "It's better for our tennis but socially it's not fun. If you want to be a tennis player, dating is secondary."

The lucky ones—Val, Chris Evert, Kristien Kemmer, Patti Hogan—had male friends in the tennis world with whom they could link up at strategic way stations on the road. Chris had met Jimmy Connors, the flamboyant twenty-one-year-old left-handed pro with the Prince Valiant haircut, in England in 1972 (they were introduced by Dick Dell, who brought Jimmy to watch Val and Chris playing doubles at a tournament), and after a year they were still going strong, much to the delight of reporters who caught them necking after practice on the courts every once in a while. Apart for much of the time, Chris and Jimmy (like Val and Dick) made it a point to visit one another during a rest week. Thus, the night Billie Jean beat Bobby Riggs in the Astrodome, Chris was not in front of a television set like the rest of the country but on a flight from Fort Lauderdale to Los Angeles, where Jimmy was playing a tournament. (She later recalled that the pilot kept announcing the scores, set by set, while the women on the plane cheered and the men sank deeper into their seats.)

For Chris and Val, such relationships were especially suitable, because, like couples in show business, journalism or other insular worlds, they could always talk shop. "It's a common bond—you've always got something to share. If I'm a housewife and he's off doing business, and he wants to share something about a deal he made, the housewife thinks, big deal. But I enjoy hearing about his tennis and he enjoys my little experiences," Val explained.

Chris and Jimmy played mixed doubles together in tournaments, and Jimmy, according to Chris, was a careful critic of her game. I sometimes wondered whether there was not something intriguingly Freudian about the women like Val, Chris and others who, having been schooled in tennis by their fathers, chose men from the same athletic mold as their boyfriends. (Indeed, all the women who spoke of their parents had grown up much closer to their fathers than their mothers, with the exception of Julie Heldman.)

Both Val and Chris insisted there was no element of competition lurking behind their relationships with male tennis players; Chris made a point of praising the cool way Jimmy handled the parade of reporters and Chris-watchers who interviewed him about her instead of about himself. But they were the exceptions. Linda Tuero, who had made history by becoming the first woman on the Tulane University tennis team, told me that Louisiana State and other all-male rival teams had refused to play against her, and that even though she was "one of the boys" on her own team, her presence had ruined at least one romance. "I was dating one of the boys. We were competing at the same time. I wanted to beat the hell out of him and he wanted to do the same with me. It didn't last very long."

Kris Kemmer, who dated Frank Froehling, one of the male pros, described intersex tennis relationships in a more complex way. She and Frank had a "rare" understanding, she said. "To be a tennis player you've got to be a little kooky, you have to feel that you're a little special, you're an egomaniac. When you have two egomaniacs sitting at one table, you can go crazy. It's also tough because if one person is down because she lost, and the other is up because he won, you can't help but be jealous, even if it's just subconscious."

With many men outside the tennis world, the situation often was worse. "As soon as men find out I'm a good tennis player, they want to start *beating* me," Julie Anthony said. "They say, 'Okay, can you play Ping-Pong? Let's play Ping-Pong. How about badminton?' And they just start challenging you. I have no desire to beat anyone in Ping-Pong or badminton, but when they come on to me like that, I want to skunk 'em!" She sighed. "I wouldn't be fierce at the Ping-Pong table if they didn't make it out to be such a duel."

Even men spectators who enjoyed watching the women play often felt threatened by them, I discovered. It was the Bobby Riggs chauvinist syndrome. Time after time men would sit in the stands, watching Billie Jean or Margaret, make admiring comments about a shot, and then, instinctively, make a crack about their chromosomes, their henpecked husbands or their looks. (Interestingly, I found that the anti-Billie Jean contingent usually couldn't decide whether they disliked her more because she had had an abortion or because they speculated she was a Lesbian. They also usually wanted to sleep with her. Talk about sexual insecurity!)

Actually, women's tennis had produced some odd intersex couples—Tuero and her boyfriend, William Peter Blatty, author of *The Exorcist,* who would sit in the stands in a Mets cap during her matches trying to put the hex on her opponents; Patti Hogan and Lance Tingay, the sixty-plus tennis writer for the London *Daily Telegraph;* Janet Young and Larry King, who spent time together at Forest Hills and whose romance gave birth to false rumors of an imminent King divorce. (It also was cited as a reason for Billie Jean's increasingly short temper.) But even more fascinating were the marriages it had produced: Larry and Billie Jean, Margaret and Barry, Wendy Gilchrist and John Paish, Nancy Richey and Ken Gunter, Carole Caldwell and Clark Graebner.

The Graebners had both been top-ranked amateurs, but soon after they married, Carole had gone into semi-retirement to have children. By all accounts, they had been a stormy combination (I never met either). According to one well-known story, Clark had taken a girlfriend to one of Carole's matches, while the Graebners were in the midst of a temporary separation. Carole got so nervous that she proceeded to throw away the match.

Wendy and John Paish were a different story entirely, a nearly stateless couple who, in their nine-month-old marriage, had not yet acquired a permanent home. John was British, Wendy, Australian. Both were touring pros, separated for weeks on end by the separate circuits. "Right after we got married I went on the Slims tour and we were away from each other for six weeks. It was awful!" Wendy said. "So we talk on the phone a lot, and we've decided that we're only going to be apart three weeks at a time now."

The Paishes kept their clothes in her parents' apartment in New York (her father was now a teaching pro in the Bronx), but they still had dozens of wedding presents in storage at friends' houses on either side of the Atlantic. "We have a car somewhere in London," she added, "but we're going to sell it because it never leaves the garage."

Nancy Gunter had solved the problem of long separations from her husband by cutting down on the number of tournaments she played. According to friends, Nancy, in her early years a taciturn, intense competitor, had become far more outgoing since her marriage.

Then there were the Kings and the Courts, the reigning sovereigns of the tennis empire, who stood out like the chieftains of warring castles in a medieval tapestry. On the surface, the Courts had a marriage made in heaven and the Kings a marriage made up by Kate Millett. In reality, both couples were revolutionary, but only the Kings would acknowledge it.

Barry Court, a big, handsome yachtsman with the rawboned appeal of a young, Australian Randolph Scott, had met Margaret in 1966, while she was running her boutique in Perth after quitting the tennis circuit. They were married a year later; he had never seen a tennis match. It had been Barry who sensed Margaret's itch to rejoin the circuit, Barry who thought it would be fun to tour the world. Now, it was Barry who baby-sat while Margaret went out to earn the family keep, Barry who sat dutifully on the sidelines while Margaret performed, Barry who amused baby Danny with a tennis ball while Margaret suited up for work in the locker room.

"We're not revolutionary, we're just like everyone else," Barry Court said in answer to a question one day. "This is the most lucrative field in the world for women, and it would be silly for Margaret not to take advantage of it." When they returned to Perth for their annual two-month vacation, he said, their roles would once against be reversed, "normal." She would cook, he would play tennis. "Margaret makes a great roast lamb, you know," he said proudly.

Margaret rarely got a chance to show off her cooking; they had been on the road almost constantly for five years. At first, Barry merely accompanied her. Then, at the start of 1973, he started helping to handle her business contracts along with a lawyer. "It's a team effort," she maintained. "Barry is the first one to tell you that if someone is gifted in something, whether it's a man or a woman, she should do it."

"The only difference between me and other men is that I'm married to Margaret," Barry maintained. "If anyone else were married to her, he'd be doing the same thing."

I could never figure out the Courts. Were they dense or was their revolutionary lifestyle really only temporary? At Forest Hills later in the summer, I half-jokingly asked Barry whether he thought a woman's place was in the home.

"Oh yes, eventually," he replied with perfect seriousness. "Especially with a lot of children."

Little Danny Court had apparently been an accident, although both parents took obvious delight in him. There was not likely to be an accident between the Kings. They were no longer living as husband and wife.

The Kings had begun, in 1965, as what Larry described as "the all-American boy-girl couple." They had met a few years earlier at Cal State, L.A., in the library,

Rosie Casals

ABOVE The Heldman women: mother Gladys, sisters Julie and Trixie
Credit: Art Seitz

BELOW The Courts, Margaret, Danny and Barry
Credit: Art Seitz

Billie Jean
and Larry King

Francoise Durr
and Topspin

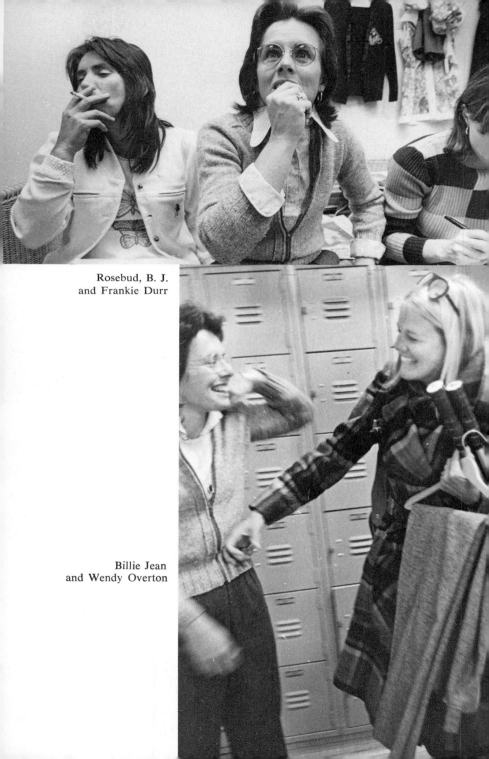

Rosebud, B. J.
and Frankie Durr

Billie Jean
and Wendy Overton

Resting: Nancy Richey Gunter
Exercising: Kathy Kuykendall
Recovering: Kristien Kemmer

Billie Jean

Evonne Goolagong
Credit: Art Seitz

Janet Newberry

Patti Hogan

Linesman on duty

gotten married, and set up a typical students' apartment in Berkeley when Larry started law school there. "Our mutual expectation was that when I got out of law school, she'd retire and have babies," Larry, an attractive, blond twenty-eight-year-old who looked like a grown-up Dennis The Menace, remembered. "We both worked part-time, Billie Jean cooked dinner every night. Then Open tennis came along, and she wasn't ready to settle down. I could have put off my career for several years and traveled with her, played a supportive role, but I couldn't do that, either. So we had our separate careers, and when people don't see each other much, the relationship has to change."

King related the story in the most even of tones, just as Billie Jean did when she spoke warmly of Larry's encouragement in the early years. "He was the one who said, 'Don't waste your talent,' " she said. "I wouldn't have been able to do it without him—he was secure, and it made me feel strong."

The Kings both were driven with ambition, she for success in tennis, he for success in business. While she toured the world playing tennis, he worked his way through law school, operating machines in factories on the overnight shift, promoting tennis tournaments, managing Billie Jean's portfolio. In the tennis world, he was considered an over-zealous "pusher," and men, especially, liked to attribute his dizzying manipulation of business ventures—World Team Tennis, Tennis America, the women's sports magazine, a management company—to overcompensation. What they didn't grasp was that behind the baby face lurked the soul of a wheeler-dealer, who loved hatching deals as much as Billie Jean loved hitting backhands.

As a businessman and as Billie Jean's business partner, he was, from all I could tell, secure enough within himself to bear the burden of a famous wife. Larry knew the public saw him merely as Billie Jean's husband. Yet not only did he show no signs of neuroticism over it, he maintained a puckish sense of humor about the idea. In Honolulu for a vacation after the Riggs match, he was introduced to a man

179

who immediately asked for his autograph. Larry jovially obliged; his signature read: "Mr. Billie Jean King."

Nobody, however, not even Billie Jean and Larry themselves, could quite make out why they did not get divorced. "We probably should have lived together before we were married," she said, "but we were hung up on Puritanism. We'd be better off divorced and living together. I'm tired of the idea that you have to stay with someone because of a contract." Larry called it a matter of "love, convenience, understanding. We've loved each other for a long time even though we're not really husband and wife," he said.

And so, they lived their separate lives. Billie Jean would come to a tournament city and rent a suite with Marilyn; if Larry passed through the same city, he'd stay in another room. If they did not get divorced, perhaps it was because the forgotten contract still gave each of them an anchor in their turbulent worlds. No longer lovers, they were the best of friends.

The younger women on the tour looked at the Kings and the Courts, the Paishes and the Graebners and wondered whether marriage might best be left to nine-to-fivers. "Marriage," said eighteen-year-old Chris Evert one day while discussing the behavior of married men who were on the road all the time, "does not seem to mix with tennis."

Being the traditionalist she was, she looked forward to settling down one day with a family, with her responsibilities limited to cooking gourmet meals and decorating the house. (In December, she and Jimmy Connors announced their formal engagement, complete with diamond ring.) But like most of the other women, she could not envision touring with a family like Margaret did. They generally agreed with Kris Kemmer, who simply put off the issue by thinking in terms of playing till she was thirty, then trading in her lace panties for her baby's Pampers. In the meantime, she said, "You realize the kind of life you're leading is fairly transitory, and if a relationship works out, great. If it doesn't, you just keep moving."

Billie Jean, on the other hand, was nearly thirty, she had had an abortion ("for a lot of reasons, all personal, which I don't want to go into, but it wasn't just because of my career"). She could understand why Margaret chose both family and the road. Nevertheless, she spoke movingly about double standards: "We're brought up to believe the place of women is in the house, and it's really screwed up a lot of women. A lot of women don't have that maternal instinct, and I think some men can raise a child a lot better than a lot of women." Billie Jean smiled when I asked if she'd still like to have children herself. "When I was younger, I thought I'd have two or three by now. Guess I better get going—I'm gettin' old!"

As Billie Jean had said, what locker room talk there was among the women about sex, love and marriage rarely got down to the "nitty-gritty." Most of them were young, inexperienced and even uptight in comparison to their peers in the outside world. Julie Heldman had mentioned that when she tried to bring up subjects such as birth control, "They think I'm dirty-minded." ("Actually"—she laughed—"I am, but I also think we have to deal realistically with our bodies.")

Lesbianism was one particular subject that was off limits, even though a small percentage of the players were gay and the others knew which ones they were. When the matter *was* brought up, it was sometimes among straight girls who gossiped about the gays behind their backs. When reporters asked about it, they were sometimes chewed out by the players, who felt they were all being cast as man-haters or man imitators by an outside world that could not cope with the idea of athletes who didn't wear jockstraps.

"If you don't date a lot, you're thought of as a Lesbian," said Kris Kemmer disgustedly. "Most of us are uptight about talking about it because we're always accused of it, and because most of the time when we're approached about it, it's like 'Ho, ho, that's perverted.' For myself, I wouldn't be interested, but I don't think anyone has a right to put somebody down for it." And that, she said, was precisely the implication the questioners had in mind.

What made it even more difficult was that many of the men pros assumed most of their female counterparts were Lesbians, and did not hesitate to say so. "The funny thing is to just turn around and say to them, 'Well, we've heard rumors about you!'" Kris Kemmer said. (According to the women, there was more homosexuality among the men players than among themselves, yet the double standard worked there, too. I was forever meeting sportswriters or fans who assumed many of the women were gay, but nobody made such an automatic judgment about the men.)

Lesbianism thus remained in the closet as far as its being a fit subject for serious adult conversation was concerned. That did not stop the players from relating juicy tales about gay (and straight) seducers. One player told me that a famous star of the 1950's had a penchant for "corrupting" young girls. When she was eight, she was invited up to the star's hotel room, alone. When she got there, the star emerged stark naked from the shower. "She didn't do anything," the player added, "but when I told my mother she warned me to stay away from her."

There were also tennis camp-followers (not true groupies in that they didn't travel with the tour) both gay and straight, who liked to hang out with the players and flirt. Sometimes they made the wrong choice. One player who was straight was confronted by a gay divorcée in whose home she was staying who demanded to kiss her good night. On the other hand, a gay player was confronted by a straight host who demanded the same privilege. There were times when I began to think nuns had an easier time finding bedmates than women tennis players.

With Madame Superstar out of the tournament, members of her supporting cast got a chance to catch some of the spotlight in the quarterfinals. Actually, for Joy Schwikert and Tory Fretz, it was only a few rays. Lesley Hunt polished off Schwikert 6-3, 6-1 in a match notable mainly for a couple of audible "Shits" from Lesley. At twenty-two, she was another young old pro, an endearing tomboy from Perth, Australia, who should have won more matches than she did. This year, she had been plagued by both tonsillitis and mononucleosis, but her more serious ailments were a weak second serve and a lack of discipline. "I'm really not a very good percentage player," she said, sighing, as we chatted in the locker room after one match. "I like the glory shots more than the bread and butter ones." Not surprisingly, the players she most liked to watch were King and Casals.

What interested me most about Lesley was the length of her "dresses." They were, in fact, shorts and a tunic top, since Lesley, like Nancy Richey Gunter, was one of the holdouts against true dresses on the court. She had gone crazy as a child with pleated tennis skirts that kept billowing up around her ears. "Besides," she added, "the only time I wore a dress was when I went to church." Now, under Teddy Tinling's guidance, her clothes were undergoing a slow but steady transformation. The first tunics she had worn early in the year came midway down her shorts; the ones she was wearing in Allaire were about two inches longer. By late in the year, Lesley's shorts had just about disappeared under the dresslike tunic. Her game had seemed to improve in the same way over the year—minutely but surely.

Kerry Harris, the girl with the crunching serve and the panties too prominent for Teddy's taste, was also improving. She had reached the Allaire quarterfinals, only to lose once again to Court. This time, however, it was not the kind of thrashing she had suffered at Margaret's hands in Philadelphia; The Arm was pressed hard before she beat Kerry 7-5, 6-4. "Kerry's one of the girls who has improved a lot," commented Barry Court. "That's the trouble— Margaret keeps waiting for an easy match and she doesn't get them anymore."

Rosie, too, had her hands full with Janet Newberry, a nineteen-year-old Floridian with braces still on her teeth who, according to the veterans, needed only a Dr. Atkins feeding schedule to propel her into the top ranks. (She was a good twenty-five pounds overweight, and was, that week, on a thousand-calorie diet.) Rosie won 6-3, 6-3. The next night, she would have to face Court again.

After the matches, Tory, Rosie, Ceci Martinez, Peachy Kellmeyer and I went out to a seafood restaurant. Tory had lost to Krantzcke; she had beer instead of champagne. (She also had the first boiled lobster of her life. When she asked what the mush in the middle was, I explained that the lobster was a lady. "You mean," she said with infinite anguish, "that I'm eating its poor ovaries?")

Casals had, among other things, a cigar. "I'm really gettin' into cigars—you don't inhale, so it's better than cigarettes," she said. As we started the drive home, Rosie was at the wheel of the lead car, a fresh Tiparillo clenched between her teeth, with me following. She promptly got us lost, and we spent the next two hours exploring the forests and wetlands of coastal New Jersey before we finally barreled into the driveway of the Essex and Sussex. Rosie staggered into the hotel, a big grin still surrounding what was now the stump of the Tiparillo, looking like an Apache who had traded all her furs for firewater. The next day, I bought the biggest, fanciest-wrapped cigar I could find, a present for the Apache if she could finally beat The Arm.

Give That Lady a Cigar

MARGARET COURT WAS SITTING IN A BIG LEATHER ARM-chair in the "interview" room, the club's office that doubled as press headquarters for the tournament. "You know that if you win the semifinal tomorrow night, you're guaranteed $3,500," Steve Lurie, the Slims PR man, told her. "That would give you $119,400 in prize money for the year. Billie Jean made $119,201 last year. You'd become the new all-time, one-year prize money leader in women's sports."

Margaret stretched out her legs and looked down at the callused big toes sticking out of her high-heeled spaghetti-strap sandals. "That's nice," she said placidly.

Someone asked if she got a special satisfaction out of topping a King record. "No," she said. "BJ's the one who made such a big fuss about money. Over the years, I've beaten her a lot more than she's beaten me." She permitted herself a smile.

Margaret stirred in the chair as if to leave, but the questions wouldn't stop. Had she given Billie Jean any advice about Riggs? Did she approve of Billie Jean accepting his challenge? Did she and Billie Jean get along?

A tiny spark of anger flashed in Margaret's cool blue eyes. "I don't know her," she replied icily. "We don't go out to dinner together, we don't go shopping together, we don't think alike. The only thing Billie Jean and I have

185

in common is tennis." She let out a small breath of air.
"Well," she said softly, "I guess that answers that!" She
stalked out of the room.

It was the closest Margaret had come to exposing the
animosity everyone on the tour knew she harbored about
Billie Jean. Billie Jean was a public person, an extrovert
who never gave a second thought to speaking her mind,
who believed that all was fair in love and tennis. Margaret
was a private person, who believed that pride should be
tempered with modesty, opinions muted by restraint.
Peachy Kellmeyer had once remarked offhandedly, "Margaret represents everything Billie Jean hates, and Billie
Jean represents everything Margaret despises." Margaret
would never express such feelings. Yet it was evident in the
way she glared disapprovingly when Billie Jean threw tantrums on court, evident in the way she avoided her in the
locker room, that every traditionalist, ladylike fiber of her
being recoiled at Billie Jean's showboating, her politicking,
her flamboyant love affair with success. For ten years,
Margaret Court had stood before the throne of women's
tennis awaiting her coronation; instead, a scrubby little
peasant from Long Beach had run off with the crown.

Later that day, I asked Margaret if, like the rest of the
Slims players, she would be at courtside in the Astrodome
September 20. "I plan," she replied sweetly, "to be out
fishing."

The next afternoon, as Rosie practiced on the main
court, about two dozen ball girls in Virginia Slims T-shirts
trooped into the empty stands to watch. They chattered ex-
citedly about Casals. A plump fourteen-year-old and a
skinny twelve-year-old argued furiously about whether Rosie
would beat Court that night. The plump girl noticed I had
a press kit in my hand, filled with glossy photos of the
players. She immediately appropriated it and everyone
grabbed for a picture of one of their favorites.

I thought back to Wimbledon, when I had asked Billie
Jean if she had had heroines as a child. "Not really," she

had answered, "because all the athletic heroes were men."
It was one reason why she was genuinely touched when
little girls approached her as they would some movie star.
In Houston, later on, just before the Riggs match, she spent
half an hour poring over a scrapbook a Texas girl had
compiled about her, and when the good-luck telegrams
poured in to her hotel suite the same week, the one that
tickled her the most was from a girls' high school basketball team in Oklahoma that praised her for giving girls
more of a chance to compete in sports. Margaret, too, responded warmly to the attentions of little girls. The afternoon of one big final on the Slims tour, she took a half
hour out of her practice time to hit with a ball girl who had
given her a wristband the girl had worn while winning a
children's tournament.

Now, I wondered if Margaret and Billie Jean would
have been amused by the dickering over the press photos.
The plump girl had wound up with pictures of both King
and Court, the skinny one with that of Casals. The plump
girl waved the pictures of King and Court at the skinny girl,
looking covetously at Rosie's photo. "Trade ya?" she asked.

Rosie was the favorite not only of the plump girl that
night, but of about 3,000 Jersey shore vacationers who
packed the stands under the high, wood-beamed ceiling of
the Allaire Racquet Club for the Casals-Court semifinal.
Rosie had played sensational tennis all week, and the fans
also realized that if she did not beat Margaret, neither
Krantzcke nor Hunt, who faced one another in the other
semi, were likely to. None of the fans disliked Margaret.
It was just that she had won eleven of the fourteen Slims
tournaments already during the year, and Rosie had won
only one—the Family Circle event with its $30,000 first-
prize check.

Rosie was the decided underdog. Since their epic battle
in Philadelphia in April, she had played Margaret only
once, in Nashville, and had lost again, 6-4, 6-2. "It's getting
to be like her Billie Jean hangup," one of her friends said.

"If she doesn't beat her now, I don't know if she ever will."

A Casals rooting section had formed in one of the front boxes behind Rosie's changeover chair, and I was in it. At the Philadelphia match she had been just a gutsy little Indian fighting the John Wayne of women's tennis. Now, she was also a friend. I was so busy screaming with the rest of the crowd when she smashed an overhead for a winner or moaning when Margaret whizzed a passing shot down the line that I had a hard time taking notes. I wondered whether I was compromising my principles as an objective reporter until I saw that everyone in the press corps sitting behind one of the glass windows in the corridor was cheering for Rosie, too.

It was like watching one of those World Series between the Dodgers and the Yankees in the *Boys of Summer* days. Each October, my fevered Brooklyn soul burned with the anticipation of a Dodger victory while a calculating voice in the back of my mind whispered the inevitability of a Yankee win. God was on the side of the Dodgers, but he always seemed to rest on the seventh day. Rosie, like the Dodgers, had come close so many times. I looked at her and prayed today would be her 1955.

The first set was all Margaret's—her ground strokes skittered over the net, her volleys crashed into the corners, winner after winner. Billie Jean once noted that despite her long experience playing Court, Rosie still didn't "use her head" against Margaret. The only way to beat her was to serve to her backhand or into her body, Billie Jean had said. You didn't lob; "Margaret loves to leap!" Someone had asked if Billie Jean had coached Rosie on how to play Margaret. "Over and over!" she exclaimed. But tonight, Casals seemed to have forgotten all her lessons. To add insult to injury, the umpire kept referring to her as "Miss Kay-Cells." Rosie didn't seem to hear him. At 5-3, she plunked herself into the wooden chair in front of us during the changeover and stared despondently into space. Behind her, the rooting section—Peachy, Stella Lachowicz, Tory, others—mirrored her gloom. Nobody said a word. In the next game, Rosie netted a volley with a vicious swish of her racquet to make it 6-3.

The next set started just as badly, with Margaret breaking Rosie's serve in the third game to make it 2-1, holding her own in the fourth for 3-1. Suddenly, something intangible began to happen. Rosie, her face registering such anger I thought she might break her racquet over her own head, put in one ace, a second ace, a brutal overhead smash, and then a stunning drive volley right at Margaret's feet to win the fifth game at love. She ripped off the next game, and the next, and the one after that, stoking the fires of her self-disgust until she was ahead 5-3.

At Wimbledon, Ann Jones had explained to me that the best women's matches were those pitting two players of such equal quality against one another that their match hinged on emotional dominance. You could sit and watch the psychological advantage swinging from one player to the other like a metronome, she said, without knowing until the last game who would win. Ann reasoned that the beauty of women's tennis lay in the fact that women were *not* physically strong enough to rear back and produce an ace in a tight spot, the way men could. They were thus forced to rely on strategy, on concentration, on their ability to get psychologically on top of the woman across the net. Neil Amdur's "levels" theory made certain women's matches explicable to me. Ann Jones's "metronome" theory—really a variation of the same idea that women's matches were won with the brain as much as the racquet—gave me a better perspective on others, such as this one.

The metronome was swinging toward Rosie.

With the score 5-3 in Casals' favor, Margaret won a point on a down-the-line passing shot. Instead of keeping the glum silence of the first set, Rosie spat out a guttural "Come ON, you idiot. . . ." She lost the game, making it 5-4, but scrambled back in the next. On set point, she caught Margaret flat-footed at the net and flicked a passing shot down her backhand alley. Margaret jumped, stretched —but the ball dribbled harmlessly off her racquet frame.

The Arm had been a few inches too short; the Apache had won the set. Rosie threw her hands up in the air like a medicine man at a war dance, crying an orgasmic "Aargh" of relief at the ceiling. The crowd leaped to its feet and cheered. "The adrenalin started flowing in the middle of that set," Rosie said afterward. "In the first, I was so pissed off. God! I couldn't stand it! I was tanking the match. I told myself, relax, you're putting too much pressure on yourself. You know, a player feels these things. You feel the atmosphere. And there comes a time, just a fleeting moment, when you get the feeling, 'Wow, she's shook, she's on the ropes.' "

Rosie had Margaret on the ropes as the third set began, but could not finish her off. Like a wounded fighter warding off his opponent with jabs after taking a bad body blow, Margaret kept Rosie at arm's length with careful passing shots and returns-of-serve. The metronome ticked faster now: 1-0, 1-1, 2-1, 2-2, 3-2, 3-3, 4-3, 4-4, 5-4. . . . (My reporter's instincts were failing me. All I could do was scrawl "WHAT A MATCH!" in crooked script in my notebook. Next to me, Dave Hirshey of the *News* had stopped taking notes too, his jaw suspended half-open.) The two women exchanged an incredibly swift series of volleys at a net face-off, Margaret winning. They stood for a few seconds grinning at each other. 5-5, 6-5, 6-6. . . . The crowd was like an elephant herd, groaning animal roars on every point. The nine-point tie breaker would decide the set.

Margaret forged ahead 2-1, 3-1, then 4-1 as a shot by Rosie hit the tape at the top of the net and then heart-breakingly dribbled back on her own side. Margaret's back-hand drive went wide: 4-2 . . . another backhand long: 4-3 . . . a Casals backhand an inch inside the alley line: 4-4. There was only one point left to play.

Margaret served, Rosie hit a good return, and then Margaret sent a hard forehand drive skimming down the line far to Rosie's left. Casals, with one last desperate effort, lunged at it.

The ball spun low off Rosie's backhand, whooshing

into the net. She knew where it was going the minute she swung and she stood there, in the backcourt, her racquet dropping out of her hands to the floor, her eyes closed, a study in utter grief. Margaret stood motionless at the net, the two of them frozen for a second, like figures caught in a movie frame. The tableau moved once more. Rosie advanced to the net, slapping a soul shake on Margaret's outstretched palm. Margaret grasped the smaller hand warmly and held it. Rosie walked to the sideline, took a slug of water from a paper cup, crumpled it and slammed it on the ground.

Wait till next year.

Rosie slouched in the "interview" room armchair, completely composed. In interviews, she usually succeeded in papering over whatever emotions were left in her by cracking jokes or by analyzing the match with clinical detachment. This time, the emotions spilled over. For a half hour, she recited her regular monologue. Then I asked if Margaret, who was still in the shower, had said anything to her in the locker room.

She darted an ironic look at me.

"Yeah. She said she felt so sorry for me, thought I shoulda won it. I said, 'So why didn't ya miss the last shot?' " Everyone laughed, but there was a pained wistfulness in her voice. "She really likes me, you know. We get along fine. And like we've had a lot of close battles and everything, and I don't think she'd *mind* losing to me. . . ." She glanced around at the dozen or so reporters in the room. "It's gonna happen, I tell ya. I *know* I'm capable of beating her, I *know* I can hit through her, I *know* I'm capable of beating her, I'm not a loser really, although"— she let out a laugh that was close to a sob—"I keep losing."

It was a heartrending, Liza Minnelli turn, if ever there was one. I reached into my pocketbook and handed her the big cigar, the one I had hoped to give her for a victory. Like a trouper, she took the cue, biting off the tip and spitting it casually into a corner. She accepted a light and flicked some ashes on the floor, Liza Minnelli imitating George Burns.

"I'll probably be playing Margaret twenty years from now," she said, putting the tough mask on again. "She'll have arthritis, and gray hair, and a cane . . . and I'm gonna get 'er!"

Margaret walked in, looking exhausted. The reporters began questioning her, but Rosie was not about to be upstaged. When Margaret momentarily misunderstood one question, Rosie took the cigar out of her mouth and waved it in Court's direction.

"This kid's out of it tonight!" she declared. "It's her mind, I'm tellin' ya, her mind is just *not* on what she's doin'. It's too much for her, to sit down here after all that emotional strain. You've just got to ask her nice *easy* questions tonight. Tell us, Margaret," she said, leaning toward Margaret with a Burnsian wave of the cigar, "how long have you been playing tennis?"

Margaret couldn't help smiling. "Rosie"—she laughed —"get lost!" Rosie stayed where she was, hogging the conversation as if somehow it would ease the hurt of the loss. Margaret was to play Lesley Hunt the following night, yet she, Rosie and everyone in the room knew that this, as Margaret put it, "should have been the real final."

The room was filled with cigar smoke. As Margaret got up to leave, one reporter asked if she was tired. Yes, she replied, shrugging, but tomorrow would be another day, another final. She'd be ready.

Rosie's dark eyes scanned the taller woman's ruddy, leathery face. "Don'tcha feel like you're havin' a letdown, Margaret?" She asked wishfully. "Don'tcha?"

Forest Hills

Prelims

THE PLAYERS HAD THEIR CHOICE OF SUFFOCATING OUTSIDE or inside. It was the first day of play at the United States Open at Forest Hills and New York was in the middle of one of those late summer heat waves that made you wish someone would invent air-conditioned underwear.

Patti Hogan sat in a dress, stockings and pumps on the veranda of the West Side Tennis Club around the corner from the entrance to the stifling ladies' locker room.

"The only way to play in this weather," Patti declared, "is to drop-shot a lot and hope your opponent expires before you do." Tory Fretz and Kris Kemmer had another solution. They disregarded Teddy's orders and went bra-less under their new "menthol green" Tinling dresses.

Billie Jean, in slacks and a sweater despite the heat, strode through the lounge and dining room inside the clubhouse behind the veranda surrounded by Marilyn, Larry, Dick Butera and a dozen newsmen. Two weeks had passed since she had pulled out of the Allaire tournament. Instead of returning to the circuit as she had promised, she had withdrawn from the following week's tournament in Newport, Rhode Island, retiring to her Hilton Head condominium for a further rest.

It didn't seem to have helped. The light-blue eyes that could twinkle with a "Zonkereno" were hard and unseeing. She looked as if she wanted to punch Ann Phillips, an over-eager young photographer trying to get pictures for *Newsweek*'s planned cover story on the Riggs match. Ann was sticking very close to her subject, tailing Billie Jean from hotel to locker room to courtside, and Billie Jean, once the best friend the press ever had, demanded that the woman be taken off the story. (She wasn't.)

An Australian newsman caught up with King on the veranda to request an interview. "No more exclusives," she snapped. "You can have all the interviews you want starting September 21. If you want something now, come to the press conference after my first match."

Marilyn stood outside the entrance to the locker room as Billie Jean disappeared inside. "Oh boy," she whispered, "it's really been something. Billie Jean just can't get a moment to herself without people bothering her. I don't know why the press doesn't understand." Realizing that Marilyn, only seven months beyond her Hollywood haircutting days, was speaking out of ignorance rather than malice, I tried to explain, gently, that the press was simply trying to do its job and that her employer, the hottest news item of the month with the exception of the White House tapes, was making that job unnecessarily difficult. "But you don't understand"—Marilyn sighed. "Billie Jean has to take *care* of herself."

A few children peered inside the door, hunting for autographs. "Did you want Billie Jean?" Marilyn asked. They nodded. She reached into her Gucci bag, pulled out a stack of index cards with "Billie Jean King" signed neatly on each one, and handed them out.

Even in the heat, the wooden bleachers in the horseshoe-shaped stadium were crowded for the first-round matches between Billie Jean and Peggy Michel, Stan Smith and Humphrey Hose. But something was missing: the gut-level, Super Bowl tension of Wimbledon.

To most American fans, Forest Hills had always been the Main Event of tennis, the climax of the tournament circuit, the spectacle that made tennis synonymous with

Labor Day the way football was synonymous with New Year's Day. The winners here would get top dollar— $25,000 each, plus a Mustang. Indeed, for the first time, thanks to a contribution from Ban Deodorant (anted up after heavy lobbying by Billie Jean and the Women's Tennis Association) the women's prize money distribution was exactly the same as the men's. Featured weekend matches would be televised nationwide, the finals would make page 1 of *The New York Times,* sportswriters from a dozen countries would file daily accounts for readers around the world. Nevertheless, the players and the press knew that no victory here would rate an extra paragraph in the record books the way one at Wimbledon would.

For the players, what Forest Hills lacked in status it made up for in raffish American charm. "I've always played better here," Kerry Melville said, "because the atmosphere is so much more relaxed. At Wimbledon, you ride out to the courts in an official car like a queen. Here, you rough it on the subway. People treat you like you're human." Chris Evert bit into a home-baked brownie in the locker room one day and grinned. "It's so great to be back in America. People in England were so *formal.* Here they come like it was a baseball game."

As a reporter and as a fan, I was comfortable at Forest Hills. I had grown up watching tennis here. I had the proper press credentials. No snooty club member minded if I commandeered a table in the clubhouse dining room for an interview. Unlike at Wimbledon, there were ice cubes for my Pepsis. Unlike at Wimbledon, the people who bought the cheapest tickets were entitled to a seat.

And yet, when reporters gathered for free booze and food in one of the sponsors' tents, it was to argue whether Bobby Riggs would be able to lob Billie Jean out of $100,000 in a few weeks, not whether Arthur Ashe could outserve Bjorn Borg in a few days. Wimbledon was in the past and Astrotennis was in the future—the U. S. Open had become just another ball game.

* * *

197

After polishing off Peggy Michel in the first round, Billie Jean spent an hour answering questions at a press conference, then another half hour after she beat Karen Krantzcke in the second round. Not one question asked at either related to the match she had just played. At one point, walking along the side courts to the clubhouse, someone asked her if she had a game plan against Riggs. "Yup," she replied, "I'm gonna beat the ass off him."

Billie Jean, Margaret and Rosie all marched without too much trouble through the first two rounds. So did Evonne and Chris, who had spent the summer fattening their bank accounts on the U.S.L.T.A. tour. The schism between the two circuits was about to end, a peace treaty having been signed earlier in the year giving the U.S.L.T.A., Virginia Slims and the Women's Tennis Association joint responsibility for setting up a unified 1974 tour, with $50,000 the minimum prize money per tournament, as compared with $25,000 on the 1973 Slims tour. The treaty also provided for a nonconflicting schedule of weekly tournaments beginning after Forest Hills, in which U.S.L.T.A. women would be allowed to play Slims events. As the price for peace, the Slims players had agreed to end their contracts with Gladys Heldman, the woman most responsible for getting the Slims circuit in gear, thus effectively ending her career as a promoter. Gladys had been wryly philosophical about the affair. "To say we were blackmailed or ransomed doesn't help the situation. Why knock what's been done? It's much better to say a truce has been made. So the U.S.L.T.A. will be running the tour in 1974. It leaves me able to go to the movies at night. Besides," she added, "I still have a magazine to run."

A few minor upsets began to break the monotony of the women's draw. Jeanne Evert, ground-stroking tenaciously on the fast, dry, unfamiliar grass surface, knocked Val Ziegenfuss out in the second round, while her mother *kvelled* on the sidelines. Jeannie had turned professional a few weeks before her sixteenth birthday, making her eligible to collect prize money. "Gosh," said Colette, "it's so wonderful to see her get a few good wins under her belt. Not for the money. For her self-confidence."

Julie Anthony, who had been touted to me as a comer at Allaire, scored an easy win over Patti Hogan when Patti threw one of her more unpleasant fits. "Patti has an insane look on her face sometimes, doesn't she?" said Julie. "It's like she's having a breakdown right on the court."

There were some poignant dramas in the men's early rounds, especially when Vijay Amritraj, a reed-thin young Indian, swept aside the aging champion Rod Laver while storm clouds thundered appropriately overhead.

For a handful of the spectators, however, the biggest drama of the early rounds centered around a tall, powerfully built older woman who strolled around the grounds like an aging actress touring a theater on whose stage she had once taken solo bows. The handful of spectators were black; the woman was Althea Gibson.

Gibson, in the late 1950's the most fearsome serve-and-volleyer in the women's game, was one of only two players to have cracked the white shell of top tournament tennis. The other was Arthur Ashe. There were a few other black players around, but none of them had made a name, and even in 1973, few seemed to give a damn about changing the situation. It was not hard to understand the absence of blacks in tennis—the game had always been played in rich or middle-class clubs, not on inner city asphalt. Nor were America's ghettos dotted with public courts the way they were with basketball hoops. Gibson and Ashe, like Jackie Robinson in baseball, had forged their way to the top in part through the sheer superiority of their talents. But no one had followed on Gibson's and Ashe's heels the way blacks had in the big league team sports.

Sports was a traditional avenue for blacks to move forward and tennis was now the prime avenue for women athletes to move forward. Why wasn't there a whole slew of new Althea Gibsons, instead of four unknown black women who played only intermittently on the Slims circuit? One of them, Sylvia Hooks, had once laughed bitterly when I asked.

"It takes money to be a tennis player, sweetheart, simple as that, and black folks don't have that kind of money. Lessons, racquets, balls, shoes, travel expenses—the black family just can't afford it for a kid the way whites can. Then the white kids who don't have money can get sponsors. But if you're black, forget it. Who wants to sponsor a black unless he's Arthur Ashe?"

A former gym teacher from East Orange, New Jersey, Sylvia had been invited to join the Slims tour at the beginning of the year by Gladys Heldman, who paid the airfare for her and several other promising blacks out of a special slush fund. The slush fund came from the circuit's prize money; the players kicked back 10 percent to pay for it and for tour officials' salaries.

Sylvia admitted freely that even with her expenses paid, she choked on the tour, winning only $430 in thirteen tournaments. "The pressure's just too much," she said. "If you don't win, you don't eat." It was not just the pressures of tournament caliber competition. In some cities, she could hear spectators pointing at her: "See, there she is, that's the one." At the Jockey Club in Miami, where the Slims held a big spring tournament, a Confederate flag flew over the court. "I said to myself, 'My God, is this 1973?'" she recalled. "I even took pictures of it to show my friends." (Billie Jean later said that if she had seen the flag, she would have refused to play.)

The slush fund kickbacks stopped when the Slims reached their peace agreement with the U.S.L.T.A. There was no longer a provision for assisting needy players, and Sylvia Hooks had no more cash to stay on tour. She was not at Forest Hills. In the 128-player men's draw, besides Ashe, there were only Wanaro N'Godrella of New Caledonia and Arthur Carrington, the winner of the black American Tennis Association national championships, who was reluctantly given a spot after making headlines by charging that tournament officials had reneged on a promise they had made to him.

Althea Gibson was at Forest Hills to play mixed doubles with Arthur Ashe, just for fun. She was forty-six years old, she held several lucrative jobs with a New Jersey tennis club and with Pepsi-Cola, and she still thought of herself as a Negro. Some of the white players, along with the blacks, felt there could be movement by the tennis establishment in encouraging an "affirmative action" program for minority players if Althea joined in pushing for it. But it was not on her priority list: "I've never been militant," she told me with a smile. "I don't believe in fights. Talent wins out." When we spoke, she was much more interested in reminiscing about her years of greatness. "During 1956 and 1957, when I was at my peak," she said at dinner one night, drawing on a Kool, "I hardly lost a match. These girls today wouldn't have had a chance against me."

She and Ashe had decided to play the mixed, she said, partly in memory of Robert W. Johnson, a black physician who had been the mentor of both of them. "Also," she added, "I sincerely feel as the only woman Negro player, I have an image to maintain to young ladies. I don't mean to be blowing any horns, but whom do they have to look up to?"

It was late one afternoon when Arthur and Althea walked onto a side court to face Marita Redondo, the half-Filipino girl, and Jean-Baptiste Chanfreau, a young Frenchman. Out of some 10,000 spectators at the Open that day, perhaps 100 were black. Every one of them seemed to be at the Gibson-Ashe match, for the rare sight—three dark-skinned professionals on a tournament tennis court at the same time. It was a sad spectacle to me. Althea, still a towering server, was no match in the quick net exchanges against the youthful agility of Marita and Jean-Baptiste. She and Ashe lost, 6-2, 6-2. A black acquaintance of mine, who had been watching with me, turned to go back to the clubhouse. "Oh well," she said, "there aren't exactly a whole lot of them for us to identify with, are there?"

The Doc

BY BEATING PATTI, JULIE ANTHONY HAD EARNED THE DUBI-
ous honor of facing Chris Evert in the third round. Sitting
in the ladies' locker room lounge the day before their Sunday match, I asked Julie what her strategy would be against
Chris.

"I'm going," she said with a warm smile, "to beat the
shit out of her."

Julie Anthony looked like the person least likely to
beat the shit out of anything. She was a slender, almost
ethereally beautiful twenty-six-year-old Californian, with
olive skin, high cheekbones and a mane of long straight
black hair. When I saw her in an ankle-length white dressing
gown one morning in Allaire, she reminded me of Claire
Bloom playing Ophelia. But on court, the sinewy muscles in
her tanned arms and legs belied the impression of frailty.
Off court, in conversation, she made the bulk of the players
sound like third graders.

Julie was a thesis away from her Ph.D. in psychology
at the University of California at Los Angeles, a scholar
who could talk as easily about the problems of mentally disturbed children as she could about serve-and-volley. She
had been a promising junior until she left tennis in 1966 to
do her undergraduate work at Stanford. In 1969 she returned briefly to the circuit to play Wimbledon, traveled
in Europe, and then devoted herself to her graduate studies.

But in 1972 and again in 1973, she began to play more tournaments, using the pro circuit as a profitable between-semesters summer job. (She had also played hookey in order to compete in three spring tournaments.) Her game was as fascinating to me as her mind, for Anthony played with an ecstatic glow about her that made non-tennis-playing spectators want to run right out and sign up for lessons. Val Ziegenfuss, Billie Jean and others had used the word *ecstasy* in describing what it felt like to hit a great shot. Julie simply exuded ecstasy on every point. She would break into a brilliant grin each time she hit a winner, flip her long ponytail up over her forehead, blow the hair away from her face, then shake her head as if she were telling herself, "God, Julie, you're so terrific!" She later explained that when she hit the ball right, "There's so much ease to it, it's like when you make a nice run in skiing and you know you've hit a few great turns. You just have to stop and laugh, almost. That's why, when playing well is coupled with winning, it's so addicting."

So far in 1973, she had come a long way for a part-timer, reaching the quarterfinals of the doubles at Wimbledon, picking up $4,275 in prize money in a handful of tournaments on the Slims circuit. The other players—even those far more experienced—did not take her lightly, because her smooth, aggressive, heady play had won her more sets than she had a right to have taken.

What was most fascinating about Julie was that she had the good fortune to live in two worlds as an athlete and as a scholar, and could articulate the relationship between them.

"I've often wondered," she said, "could I enjoy my summers as much if I knew that I would have to play tennis all year round? Knowing I have to go back to school—does that make me run around harder, as though I have to take a last gulp of air before I have to dive down into school again? And what about vice versa? Could I apply myself as diligently to school knowing there wasn't going to be a break where I could get out in the fresh air? I've often realized that tennis and psychology are the two therapeutic aspects to my life. One is therapy for the tensions of the other."

There were not many players on the tour who felt the need for a mental release from their tennis tensions. Most of them were physical persons who found release in other physical activities—golf, running, swimming. Some of the players were never seen in close proximity to a book or a magazine. (Goolagong, for instance. When, at Wimbledon, Bud Collins gave Vic Edwards two copies of a book he'd written, one for Evonne, the other for Janet Young, Vic laughed and said, "You *know* that one of these isn't going to be opened!") A large number of them loved to recall how much they had hated both school and any other activity that kept them indoors. ("I worked in a bank once," Wendy Paish said, "and I used to get caught with my head out the window all the time.")

When she first toured as a junior, Julie Anthony, like Julie Heldman, discovered she was something of a freak to her athletic colleagues, and another kind of freak to her egghead friends. "In the juniors," she remembered, "we used to live in dormitories and the girls would have balloon fights while I sat on my bunk reading. Val Ziegenfuss told me later she felt so sorry for me. They never realized that I *liked* reading." Fellow psychology students, on the other hand, were always surprised to find out that she was a tennis pro on the side.

This year, though, "Doc" Anthony, as the press quickly nicknamed her, had discovered that players she might once have dismissed as mere jocks were now interesting people to her.

"I have the luxury of being able to know a lot of different people—people pigeonholed in their office doing research and people like Pancho Gonzalez," she explained, without a trace of snobbishness. "And what's interesting is that they aren't that dissimilar. There are parallels, commonalities of people who are good in their fields no matter what they are. Things like attention and concentration and perseverance. Doing esoteric research and being a great football player are more similar than you think."

One time, Julie and Ceci Martinez, another psychology major who had graduated from San Francisco State College, had spent an hour in the locker room discussing the nature of competition. Both of them studied yoga, and both related it to a kind of gratification athletes understood intuitively but rarely expressed verbally: the idea of self-mastery. "I got interested in yoga because of the parallels between its philosophy and some in psychology, like Gestalt therapy," Julie said. "That's one reason why I'm back in tennis, to try and resolve in my own mind how much control you can exert over your body via the mind. The thrill in tennis is being able to sit down, plot out a strategy, and be able to do it on court, whether it's Court 800 with nobody watching or on Court One in front of a thousand people. It's the idea of being able to train your attention, your concentration, and focus it, and then turn it off when you don't need it any more."

Chris Evert and Billie Jean King didn't express such profundities in conversation; they just went out on the court each day and demonstrated them. Julie could apply her psychology to the limit of her skill, as she had done against Patti: Hogan had fumed, and Julie had simply focused a little more carefully on each shot. Ceci, unfortunately, usually brought her yogic principles to bear in post-match seances. After one hard-fought loss in New Jersey, she had disappeared in the locker room, prepared for a rigorous three-set thinking session first in the sauna, then the whirlpool bath, then the shower. At 1 A.M. the same night I found her sitting cross-legged on the lawn of the house she was staying at, in the pitch-black darkness, sunglasses perched on her nose, a cigarette dangling from her fingers. When I asked what she was doing, she gave me a big lopsided grin. "Meditating."

Chris and Julie played in the stadium on the first Sunday of the Open, with the television cameras grinding. The humid, polluted heat had become a prime topic of concern among the players, men and women alike. Even Chris was sweating. She had taken to swallowing spoonfuls of honey before each match to keep her strength up. "I'm surprised there haven't been more defaults," she said to her friend Janet Haas. "Come on," protested Janet, "you're a tennis player. You're supposed to be in condition."

"Yeah, but this is murder," sighed Chris. "At least in Florida we get a *breeze* sometimes."

The only breezes on the stadium court that afternoon were the ones Julie Anthony's racquet made flailing at Chris's passing shots. Nobody expected Julie to win, but she put up a magnificent battle in losing. More importantly, the fans in the bleachers and on television discovered a potential new star. By the next day, everyone was talking about the charming, gracious Doc who dared to trade dropshots with Cool Chris, and who smiled as she hit them.

The Greek chorus of doomsters who had droned on at Wimbledon about Chris's demise were silent at Forest Hills. Her climb to the finals at the All-England Club had made it clear she was no shooting star, but a permanent fixture on the women's tennis horizon.

The weekend before Forest Hills, while the Slims group had played a tournament in Newport, Rhode Island, Chris had led the United States to an easy team victory over Britain in the Wightman Cup competition—a victory that was highlighted by Evert's 6-2, 6-4 trouncing of Virginia Wade. The Wightman Cup was a traditional best-of-seven series of matches between squads of five women that was supposed to be the women's equivalent of the Davis Cup. It was not, partly because it involved only two countries and partly because outside of Evert and Wade, neither country fielded a terribly interesting team. (The Americans, besides Chris, were Hogan, Redondo, Tuero and Jeanne Evert. The U.S.L.T.A., which chose the players, contended none of the top Slims such as Billie Jean could participate because they were under contract to play Newport. Billie Jean said she wouldn't play in any case because the U.S.L.T.A. hid its greediness under a cloak of patriotism and wouldn't tell her what it did with the money it made from the event.)

Although the Cup matches at the Longwood Cricket Club outside Boston had been fairly dull, Chris, the feature attraction whose face could be seen for blocks on a gigantic poster outside the club gates, had played impressively. She was coming to the net with more assurance, finishing off points more quickly by shooting for more winners, brightening up her stage presence with bright red nail polish.

Nevertheless, even this week at Forest Hills, the site of her first dazzling entrance on the major league tennis scene two years before, Chris was not given quite the same adoring reception that she had been treated to when she was, in Gene Scott's words, "The sixteen-year-old Virgin Princess." After a previous match, the fans had mobbed her, torn off her hat and stepped on her sweater in an attempt to get her autograph. When she chided them for their rudeness, they muttered that she was stuck-up.

Here, as Julie gamely hung in 3-3, in the second set after dropping the first 6-4, the crowd whistled as much for the Doc as for the Dolly. Chris won the match 6-4, 6-4; her placements had been too unerring, Julie's first serve too erratic.

In the interview room, Chris calmly analyzed her game. The reporters took desultory notes. Julie cracked jokes: the reporters grinned and scribbled. Chris, it had been determined during the questioning, was close to the $100,000 mark in prize money and had decided not to go to college. Julie, asked for a comment, declared, "In a few years, Chris will just go out and *buy* a college." Everyone howled. Once again, a bit of flash had momentarily eclipsed Chris the cool.

Partners

THE SINGLES MATCHES WERE GETTING INTERESTING. JULIE Heldman, who had gone on a rampage in Newport, beating Julie Anthony, Laura Rossouw, Rosie Casals and Kerry Melville before losing in the finals to Margaret Court, was scheduled to play Billie Jean in a third-round contest on Monday. Meanwhile, the doubles had gotten started, and I found myself drawn to them, intrigued by the four-way interplay of personalities with whom I had become familiar.

Women's doubles had few fans. Knowledgeable sportswriters claimed the matches were boring, because the women could not equal the awesome rapid-fire net exchanges that made men's doubles fun. The prize money for women's doubles was usually pitiful, except at Forest Hills where another sponsor, Fabergé, had made a contribution to equal the men's doubles prizes: $4,000 to the winning team, $2,000 to the runner-up.

In the top tournaments, most of the leading women players entered the doubles draw, although some, like Court, skipped doubles at lesser tournaments late in the summer to save their strength. There were a few teams that had been together for years, like Rosie and Billie Jean, many that had only been working together a few months, some that joined up only for an occasional tournament. Watching the doubles draw week after week was like watching partners constantly changing in a square dance.

208

The Forest Hills draw held some surprises. Chris Evert, who had played with Jeanne in the spring and with Marita in the Wightman Cup, was now teamed up with Olga Morozova, the quiet but talented Russian star. It was a shrewd business arrangement. Neither Chris nor Jeanne was at her best on grass, Olga was, and with a good grass-court player Chris could get much further up the doubles ladder. (For the Wightman Cup the previous week, Jeanne, curiously enough, had been teamed with Patti Hogan, whose antics had so infuriated her earlier in the year.) In another switch, Lesley Hunt, who during the spring had played with Court, was now teamed with Martina Navratilova, while Court was back with Virginia Wade, her Wimbledon partner.

Martina and Lesley played Rosie and Billie Jean late one afternoon in a misty rain that made the grass so slick the players kept losing their footing. There were so many pratfalls the match began to look like a Laurel and Hardy movie.

King and Casals had been partners for such a long time that it was almost as if an invisible wire stretched between them, swinging them into a perfect pattern on every shot. Navratilova and Hunt acted like a couple in bed together for the first time; they knew the right moves, but they kept on getting tangled up in awkward positions.

The way the players described it, finding the right doubles combination was a little bit like making a good marriage. "You have to get along with your partner—you have to be a team," Betty Stove, who was considered one of the great doubles players, explained. "You have to be able to accept each other's mistakes."

Having played for a year with Francoise Durr, Betty added that she could almost feel, without looking, where Francoise was on the court at a given moment. In addition, their styles complemented one another. Francoise was a self-taught finesse player whose elbows and knuckles stuck out in every direction when she hit the ball, but she had pinpoint accuracy that would have made Minnesota Fats envious.

Betty, who was built along the lines of a pulling guard and who enjoyed cigars as much as Rosie did, was a power player with a murderous overhead.

Betty was one of several players who admitted she enjoyed doubles better than singles, because of the teamwork involved. Val Ziegenfuss was another. One reason she had had most of her big wins in doubles, Val said, was because she preferred the idea of a team sport. "Maybe it's coming from a basketball family, but I love the idea of two of us out there together, sharing." Some doubles combinations simply clicked the first time on court together, Val said. That was how it was now that she was playing with Peggy Michel. "It's respect for one another, faith in one another, having that sense of dependability, confidence that she's going to come through even if I miss and vice versa." In contrast, she said, when she had played briefly with another friend, Chris Evert, "we were simply two singles players on the same side. It didn't work."

Doubles partners not infrequently went through what amounted to short-lived romances, divorces, remarriages. Val and Wendy Overton had split up their team because they found they could not room together on the road, play doubles together, and then play their best against one another in singles. After winning nearly every doubles title in tennis, Billie Jean and Rosie had broken up their combination for a time, because, in Rosie's words, "It wasn't any fun anymore," and also, according to friends, because Rosie had become so dominated by Billie Jean's personality their relationship had blocked her progress as a championship singles player.

Back together again this year, King and Casals had resumed their winning ways. They beat Hunt and Navratilova handily and eventually went on to reach the finals before losing to Court and Wade. But by the time the week was finished the draw had produced some wonderful match-ups. There was, for instance, Doc Anthony and the Marengo Kid—Julie Anthony and Mona Shallau—who looked like a pair of terriers in their identical yellow-and-blue Head dresses. They put up a lovely battle against Rosie and Billie Jean, hugging each other when one of them made a great shot, giggling together on lucky net cord dribblers, and radiating a general joie de vivre that gave the fans their money's worth. In contrast, there was a memorable match involving Patti Hogan and Sharon Walsh against Karen Krantzcke and Wendy Overton with enough screams, racquet-throwings and arguments to convince one spectator he had stumbled on the intramurals of the Bellevue psycho ward.

While Chris Evert was threading her way through Julie Anthony in the third round, Virginia Wade was, much to her distress, methodically eliminating from the tournament two of the promising young British girls she had coached as playing captain of the Wightman Cup team only a week earlier.

"I really hate having to play my friends, or someone who's been on a team with me," she said with dispassionate annoyance at lunch one day. "I can't concentrate at all. That's one of the reasons why I have never really been very close friends with any of the girls."

To hear some of the others tell it, Virginia would have had a difficult time being friends with them, period. A twenty-seven-year-old university graduate with a degree in mathematics, Wade was a loner, a mystery woman who flitted in and out of the international tennis circuit like a firefly, casting off glimmers of phosphorescent brilliance when she did play. Her favorite dress, a plain white outfit with startling scalloped edges on the bottom that were bright pink on the underside, was Teddy Tinling's finest creation, in that it conveyed the wearer's personality in one glance. "Virginia is terribly close to the establishment, on the face of it, and wants to look like a virgin, like everybody's darling, but underneath she's a tigress who wants to show off like mad," he confided.

Wade had won the Open at Forest Hills in 1968 and would have liked to win it again this year, but there was something in the way her cunning green cat's eyes haughtily surveyed the dining room that suggested she would not break her neck to do so. Virginia was the æsthete of women's tennis, the player who freely acknowledged, "I hate losing but I can't make myself win at any cost. I'd rather play beautiful tennis than win." Even her outbursts of temperament on court were beautiful, and she was well aware of their effect. "I wear my heart on my sleeve, and the fans don't mind, because they know what I'm feeling, which I think is very important. Nobody wants to love you if you're ice cold."

Fire and ice: Wade conjured up all kinds of contrasts. She spoke eloquently about enjoying Wightman Cup play because "tennis is such a selfish game it's good to have the discipline of being on a team, on somebody else's side." Yet, she was regarded by others as a less-than-selfless doubles partner and a halfhearted Women's Tennis Association officer. (At Wimbledon, she had been chosen vice chairwoman of the union, and then promptly informed the group she could not chair her assigned subcommittee meetings that week because there was so much pressure on her as Wimbledon's perennial Great White British Hope. "Jeez, who does she think she is, Queen Elizabeth?" remarked one of the American players.)

Virginia met her demise at Forest Hills in the quarterfinals against an opponent as cool as she was hot—Margaret Court, her doubles partner. The score was 7-6, 7-6, both sets having been decided by tie breakers.

Virginia, who had the strongest serve in women's tennis (Chris Evert said that in the first couple of games of a match against Wade she had to fight the urge to duck), treated the crowd to a crunching, emotion-charged performance, using the serve to keep Margaret away from the net as much as she could. On forehand drives, Wade did not swing her racquet, she uncoiled it. On her overheads, she showed her teeth, slamming at the ball like a lion-tamer snapping a whip.

Margaret was simply Margaret, invincible as Stengel's

Yankees and just as unlovable. While Virginia's game alternately blazed and fizzled like a bonfire, Margaret's glowed steadily like an electric hot plate. The end result was inevitable. I was reminded of a conversation I had had with David Gray of the *Guardian,* one of the finest tennis writers in Britain and a friend of Virginia's, who had described tennis first by paraphrasing Maréchal Foch on war: "It is not an exact science but a great emotional drama." Then David had added, "Ultimately, it is a game of reduction—one player makes the other surrender."

At the U. S. Open, as at so many other tour stops, Margaret Court had begun to force the best players in the world to drop their guns and come to the net, hands up.

Heat Wave

SOMETHING WAS VERY WRONG WITH BILLIE JEAN KING. Marilyn Barnett, sitting, to everyone's astonishment, right beside the umpire's chair on Court 22 in a spot usually out-of-bounds to all but the players and ball boys involved in a match, knew it. Larry King, watching from a table on the veranda, knew it. And Julie Heldman, poised on the other side of the net, knew it too.

Most of the Labor Day crowd of more than 11,000 that had come out to Queens in the suffocating 96-degree heat did not know it—yet. The third-round match between King and Heldman had been shunted to the obscure, pitted court in front of the noisy clubhouse terrace so that Vijay Amritraj and Allan Stone, two near unknowns, could play in the stadium. Billie Jean had gotten angry when she learned about it. She was the top seed and the main attraction at the Open—what was she doing in left field? But her anger did no good. It merely added to two other problems, which she had carefully kept secret from the prying press. Her knee, the one she had stretched in New Jersey, was bothering her despite the weight-lifting program Dr. Nicholas had prescribed. And a stubborn virus that had gripped her earlier in the week, killing her appetite and forcing her to take energy-sapping penicillin shots, was sending dizzying shivers through her body.

Only a few hundred fans had been able to find a spot

214

on the narrow walkway behind the court as their match started. Billie Jean, grim and determined, the beads of perspiration pimpling her forehead, had plowed her way through the first set 6-3, then halfway through the second until it was 4-1. The crowd had begun to drift away back toward the stadium.

Now, as she came to the sideline for the changeover, she suddenly mumbled, "I think I'm going to faint."

Julie, two games away from defeat, asked her if she wanted to quit. "I'd better play," Billie Jean said.

She walked back onto the court on rubbery legs. Like a zombie, she stood dazed as Julie's balls zipped past her. Her serve blooped weakly over the net. A quarter of an hour later, the set was Julie's, 6-4.

The word spread like electricity through the surrounding courts to the stadium: Billie Jean's in trouble. The fans began to dash back toward the clubhouse, reporters alongside them. Bud Collins, a bon vivant sportswriter who made a ritual of dining inside the clubhouse each noontime no matter who was playing, rushed out onto the veranda.

Billie Jean, no longer bothering to make a stab at balls beyond her immediate reach, began waiting longer and longer at the changeovers. It was no use. The score was 4-1 for Julie in the third.

Finally, Julie, who later told everyone gleefully that her won-lost record against King over the years was 2 to 436, got impatient. They were pros who were supposed to play by the rules, and the rules were that a player could not take more than a minute's rest during changeovers. In the discussion that followed the match, King supporters declared angrily that nobody but Julie, who didn't get along with Billie Jean and was a rat besides, would have demanded the rule enforced against an ailing opponent. Heldman supporters retorted that perhaps only one player would have—Billie Jean. King was known to be a lousy, ungracious loser.

Heldman looked up at the umpire. "Is a minute up?" she asked. The umpire didn't have a chance to reply. A gaunt Billie Jean hissed, "If you want it that badly, you can have it," snatched up her sweater and stumbled toward the locker room.

The match was over, by default. Billie Jean, who had hoped to retain her 1972 Open singles title with a smashing victory that would stand as a headline-making prelude to the Riggs match, had instead withdrawn from her third tournament in a row.

In Las Vegas, Jimmy "The Greek" Snyder hung up on his long-distance caller and quietly changed the odds on the Riggs-King match from 3 to 2 to 5 to 2. The Bobby boom was blossoming.

Kris Kemmer, another casualty of the third round (she had lost to Rosie in three tough sets), smiled on the veranda a few days later when someone passed on the latest piece of gossip, that Billie Jean was about to call off the Riggs match.

"When the time comes," said Kris, "she'll be ready. Up here"—she pointed to her head—"and physically."

Kris had a personal reason for believing in Billie Jean. Billie Jean had believed in her, when Kris had given up believing in herself.

At twenty-one, Kris already had three years as a Slims pro under her belt. She had been eager to join the tour in 1971, fresh from a string of junior triumphs, a nimble left-hander from San Diego with a two-handed backhand. Instead, she had found it a disaster. The traveling wore her down. She discovered that she couldn't drop by a friend's house when she got depressed because the friends were in California and she was usually a half-continent away. She started to lose, regularly, to the seeds and the qualifiers alike. "Boy, was my head messed up," she recalled as we chatted one day in a friend's spacious Central Park West apartment where she was staying during the Open. "All I could say was 'I can't do this, I can't beat these people.' "

She finally hit bottom in Denver in 1972. "I got

216

psychosomatic bronchitis. I called my parents, and I said, 'I'm in Denver, I'm sick, and I don't care.' " She quit the circuit without telling anyone where she was going, and hid out at La Costa, near San Diego.

Somehow, Billie Jean found out where she was. "She called me and said, 'Hey, what's the matter?' When I told her, she said, 'We've got to get your head together.' " Billie Jean knew Kris liked to keep a diary as a therapeutic exercise; she made her start writing again. She urged her to take a few months off, to practice, to think positively. When Kris rejoined the circuit in January, 1973, Billie Jean made it a point to practice with her, always talking, talking, talking about being a winner. Kris went on a vegetarian diet, took up yoga, read Ralph Waldo Emerson's essay on self-reliance . . . and began to win. She started the year as a qualifier; by September she was an occasional seed. In all of 1972 she had won not quite $3,000 on the Slims circuit. By the time the circuit ended in October, her 1973 earnings had mushroomed to over $13,000.

"I simply decided to play tennis. I told myself, 'I'm not going to say I'm not doing well.' I'm gonna say, 'No matter what, I can beat anybody I play.' " She paused. "In some ways, if it hadn't been for Billie Jean, I wouldn't be where I am today."

Two months after we talked, Kris repeated those words at a press luncheon in New York. She had just been named the winner of a $5,000 prize from Max-Pax as the most improved player on the Slims tour. Billie Jean presented her with the check, standing behind an antipasto-laden table in a wine cellar banquet room at Mamma Leone's Restaurant. As Kris burst into sobs, Billie Jean patted her streaked honey-blonde pageboy and said cheerfully, "Hey, a woman athlete's not supposed to cry!"

If I had heard the Kris Kemmer comeback story earlier, I would probably have dismissed it as a steal from *True Confessions.* But I had heard variations on the theme from a half-dozen other players who had been the object of King pep talks—Rosie, Tory, Janet Newberry among them. (Tory had remembered getting telephone calls from London from Billie Jean practically every day she had been in the hospital for her knee operation.) The way her friends told it, Billie Jean really was a jock Billy Graham, evangelizing anyone she could find with her winning-is-good gospel.

Billie Jean would give the shirt off her back to friends, according to Kris, or more specifically, the racquet out of her bag. Like all the players, King was very fussy about her racquets, sometimes switching from a tighter- to a looser-strung one in the middle of a match if things weren't going right. But if Kris wasn't satisfied with any of hers, she could always count on borrowing one from Billie Jean. (Naturally, Kris used the BJK autograph model Wilson. So did Chris Evert until Wilson started to make Chris's own model.) And in one tournament, Billie Jean borrowed a brand-new one from Kris. "She won the match and threw it up in the air," Kris remembered with a laugh, "and all I could think of was, 'Oh my God, my new racquet!' "

As it happened, racquets and suitcases were the bane of the women pros' life in terms of traveling for months on the road. Kris Kemmer and Laura Rossouw, a South African girl, who were staying together in New York, counted seventeen racquets between them when they arrived for the Open. The players always carried the racquets in their arms (not many would even let hotel porters touch them), which meant that each week they spent up to $20 in tips for porters at hotels and airports who lugged the rest of their gear. Even when a player was toting the usual complement of six racquets, her baggage was considerable. Chris Evert, for instance, usually had two huge suitcases with her on long trips—one for her tennis clothes, one for her regular clothes—plus a train case stuffed with makeup, and a handbag. Moreover, no matter how many bags they carried, the players soon got terribly bored with wearing the same outfits week after week. Kemmer solved the problem by buying new clothes in good shopping cities like

Paris and New York, and then sending a suitcase full of the old ones back to her parents in California.

The players who tried to travel light saved some porters' expenses but had a new problem: laundry. Everyone had a tale about having to leave half her underwear in Nashville or Indianapolis because a hotel had not gotten the laundry shipment before her plane left. The alternative, of course, was to do it themselves. Late one night at a tournament, I noticed Lesley Hunt standing by the club's laundry room, waiting for the tunic she had just worn in her semifinal match to come out of the dryer. "I'm only carrying three dresses with me," she explained. "The other two are dirty, and if I hadn't washed this one I'd have to play the final in my track suit!"

Among the lessons Kris Kemmer had learned on the tour was that there are no excuses in pro tennis. When I ran into her on the terrace on Tuesday, the day after Billie Jean's default and Kris's own loss to Rosie, I said "Bad luck," the traditional tennis greeting for a player who had been defeated. Kris shrugged her shoulders. "She played better than I did," she replied. When I offered the same condolences to Sharon Walsh after her doubles debacle, she answered, "It wasn't luck. I blew it." I had once told Billie Jean what intrigued me about tennis was the fact that there were no second chances in a tournament. "Your ass is always on the line," I said. "What a great phrase!" she shrieked. "That's it! That's what's so exciting about it! That's what makes it so much fun!"

Billie Jean was offering no excuses despite her default, but it hadn't done anything to improve her disposition. For the rest of the week, she moped around the clubhouse, avoided the press and regained enough strength to continue in the doubles with Rosie and the mixed doubles with Owen Davidson, winning the latter crown. The spotlight, however, had shifted temporarily to her conqueror.

Wednesday afternoon, with the temperatures only slightly above 90 now, the seats in the grandstand, a smaller arena off to the side of the big stadium right beside the Long Island Railroad tracks, filled quickly to see Heldman square off against Helga Masthoff, the woman I had chauffeured to the St. Petersburg airport. Helga, making her first appearance in ten years at Forest Hills, had beaten Olga Morozova, the Number 8 seed, to reach the quarterfinal berth. Now the crowd, totally unfamiliar with her game and her reputation for "taking points," rooted mightily for her to humble Julie the King-killer. Julie, unable to shut out the crowd's show of hatred, made it easy for her. After dropping the first set 6-3, she went totally to pieces, playing, in Rosie Casals' words, "like a scrubwoman."

A pack of the women players were in the stands, watching the match with much interest and little pity. "Oh, Julie," clucked Virginia Wade in her best upper-crust tone, as Heldman made an error, "that was so terrible. Look at her," she said to Betty Stove. "Her whole body is rigid."

At 4-1 Masthoff in the second set, not even Julie herself could summon up any pity for the way she was playing—she even applauded herself derisively when she hit one of many bad overheads. As the two women changed sides, Betty Stove turned to Virginia Wade and said dryly, "Well, now that it's 4-1 maybe *Julie* will feel faint and default."

Queen for a Day

WHAT TENSION THERE HAD BEEN IN THE WOMEN'S SINGLES draw snapped when Billie Jean defaulted. By the end of the week, so had the heat wave. The sky cleared, a wind whipped up, and the semifinals and finals were played on perfect, bright, sunny New York late summer afternoons.

The one surprise in later women's matches was Helga Masthoff, who, after booting Julie 6-3, 6-3, found herself in the semis against Goolagong, the Number 4 seed. Evonne had knocked out fifth-seeded Kerry Melville in a match that had a rodeo look about it—both women wore cowgirl bandanas around their necks to sop up the sweat.

Chris Evert, the Number 3 seed, had moved into the semis by whipping Rosie even more severely than she had at Wimbledon, 6-1, 7-5. When the two of them had begun warming up on the stadium court nearest the awning-shaded marquee, Rosie had taken one disgusted look at the pothole-sized divots in the grass just behind the baseline that had been dug up by previous players and demanded the match be moved to one of the horseshoe's two other courts. (The pros, especially men, often dragged one foot as they came down on a serve, wearing out the leather on the toe of one sneaker when they played on hard surfaces, wearing out the baseline when they played on grass.)

Mike Blanchard, the tournament referee, obliged by switching the match to the far court, but right from the beginning, even without the divots, Rosie was in a hole.

It was another one of those ulcerous battles that made me question whether I had the intestinal fortitude to be a sportswriter, a question reinforced by the cramps I got gobbling one of the West Side Tennis Club's greasy hot dogs. (The next day I wisely had yogurt instead, Forest Hills being the only major league sporting arena I knew of that had a Dannon concession stand.) Rosie, whom I was rooting for, seemed totally "psyched out" by Chris, and she was getting some bad line calls besides. Chris, whom I was also rooting for, was playing a tactical game worthy of Bobby Fischer, plotting openings by shoving low balls at Rosie's feet in no-man's-land around midcourt, then taking Casals right off the board with crisp passing shots or lovely, arcing lobs. After it was over Rosie, who had belittled Chris at Wimbledon, grudgingly paid her respects. "The kid's all right," she said.

The Kid was now the only real obstacle that stood between Margaret Court and another $25,000. No one doubted that Evonne would get by Masthoff in their semi and thus enter her first U. S. Open final. Not too many knowledgeable observers doubted, either, that Margaret could beat her there. First, however, Court had to make Chris pay for Wimbledon.

Before the match began at noon on Friday, Chris, sporting a hot-pink dress with white trim, conceded that she was worried about Margaret's serve. It had been "on," all week, pounding like howitzer shells into the green potato fields that Forest Hills passed off as tennis lawns. For the first game of the first set, Court's serve seemed to be off. Chris broke immediately, then won her own first service at love. For a brief moment, the fans sniffed an upset. At Wimbledon, they had cried, "Come on, Margaret," but princesses, not queens, were the favorites at Forest Hills. "Come on, Chrissie!" a fat, redheaded man bellowed in front of me. (Evonne Goolagong, giggling later about shouts of "Yay, Goolie," at her matches, remarked, "Sometimes here I feel like I'm in a football match.")

In the third game, the howitzers began finding their range, and Margaret moved in front, carefully waiting at the baseline until she got the right shot on which to storm the net. Court took the first set 7-5.

At each changeover, she would take deep swigs from a big bottle of Gatorade sitting under the umpire's chair. By the middle of the second, a ball boy had to come jogging out of the stands with a second bottle. I wondered idly if perhaps she was getting waterlogged, because Chris took the second set 6-2. She wasn't. Everything fell into place in the third set—beautiful dropshots, textbook volleys, more howitzers. This time, this tournament, Margaret had one of the tennis kingdom's most bejeweled crowns in sight, and no Florida schoolgirl was going to deny her it. The match ended 7-5, 2-6, 6-2, Court.

There was a graciousness about Margaret in victory that afternoon that won me over in a way the letter-perfect tennis she had played all week had not. Sitting under the stands in the pressroom after the match, someone had asked Chris if the shouts of the spectators had disturbed her concentration. "Well," Chris answered slowly, not wanting to seem ungrateful, "when the crowd goes wild . . ."

". . . and the wind starts blowing," Margaret chimed in sympathetically, "and the airplanes fly overhead . . ." She glanced rather affectionately at the younger girl. "I think Chris played very well, actually," she declared. When someone asked her about Evonne, her finals opponent, she replied, "She's a beautiful mover, isn't she?" My thoughts floated back to Billie Jean, and how, if she had been in Margaret's place, she would have talked about such opponents. Unquestionably, she would have made it clear above all else that she intended to beat the living daylights out of Evonne. Margaret intended to do the same, yet she had a classy way of not putting it in those terms.

Just as I could never become a Yankee fan, I would never be a Court fan. But I was becoming an admirer.

It took Evonne three sets to send Masthoff back to Germany. "I *do* tend to slip away in the second set," Goolie said later, giggling. Helga was already thinking about the airport. "I sought I vould lose in ze second round," she exclaimed. "I've packed sree times!"

The Court-Goolagong final was held at noon on Saturday, the first match in the stadium before the men's semis. The scheduling was significant—the stands did not get really filled each day until after 1 P.M. and the television coverage did not begin until 4 P.M. The prize money might have been equalized for the women at Forest Hills this year, but the exposure was not.

In contrast to finals day at Wimbledon, the only hats visible at Forest Hills were the Planters Peanuts visors hundreds of the fans wore—to those sitting on one side of the horseshoe, the other side looked as if it were filled with rows of beaked ducks. Also in contrast to Wimbledon, where photographers were kept completely off the hallowed turf, a score of live and still cameramen lined up parallel with the stadium's center court sideline. Others took up positions against the wall in back of the baseline until tournament director Bill Talbert, dressed like a black militant in red pants, green shirt and black belt, shooed them away.

Promptly at 12 o'clock, Evonne and Margaret strode out of the marquee onto the grass, each carrying bouquets of roses. Their personalities showed through even in their walks—Margaret's the now-familiar, stately processional, Evonne's a bouncy, cocky, head-tossing strut. Much earlier in the tournament, I had come across the two of them practicing together early in the morning. Although they were frequent rivals, Evonne and Margaret had a mentor-pupil friendship of long standing. Court, nine years older, had been Evonne's idol as a child. A faded picture of the curly-haired little aboriginal staring up worshipfully at the older woman, already a world champion, still hung on the wall of the Goolagong home in Barellan. They had, on occasion, been doubles partners.

This would not be one of David Gray's "great emotional dramas." It was more like a hard-fought but basically pleasant family tussle.

Evonne, serving first, began and ended the initial game sensationally, with aces. She was dressed in white, as usual (even though Forest Hills welcomed color costumes), appealingly sexy without a sexy girl's build. (Vic Edwards, according to reliable reports, had taken note of Evonne's figure by telling her new dress designer, "Just do what you've been doing on dresses, but back to front—she's got no titties and big shoulder blades.") She broke Margaret in the second game, hitting winners on her return-of-serve, putting her ground strokes deep toward the baseline. But in the seventh game, Margaret, who seemed to have been slow in warming up, broke back, and they stayed even until 5-5, when Margaret got a second break. All she had to do was hold her own serve in the next game to win the set.

At Wimbledon, Billie Jean had noted with some distress that Evonne could play mediocre tennis right up until it was time for her opponent to take the set, and then suddenly raise the level of her game 1000 percent. She did it now, taking the game on Margaret's serve to pull even at 6-6, and force the tie breaker. The crowd grew hushed.

Just as quickly as she had climbed that 1000 percent, she toppled back 999. On the first point, she hit an easy overhead long, on the second she double-faulted, on the third Margaret caught her flat-footed with a dropshot. Evonne picked up the next two points, then sent a forehand wide and a backhand into the net to lose the set.

In the second set, Evonne again raced from brilliance to mediocrity without ever crossing middle ground. Each time she missed a first serve, Margaret would cream her weak second one. Yet Evonne's backhand volley was cutting through balls at the net like a buzz saw, well enough for her to stay even with Court to 5-5. In the next game, on break point, she stunned Margaret with a whistling return-of-serve that pushed Court far into a corner. Margaret barely managed to get her backhand on it, blooping the ball right down the middle of the court. Evonne, on her toes at the net, volleyed it away. She won the set on the next game, to shouts of "Come on, Goolie!"

It turned out to be her last hurrah. While Evonne

bobbed around like a cork, Margaret let the superbly trained machine that was her body do its precision work. With the score 4-2 in her favor in the third set, there was no stopping Big Mama. She won eight of the final nine points, the set, the match, the title, the $25,000, the Mustang, and one silent salute from a Dodger fan in the third row of the bleachers.

The interview room looked like the IRT Express at rush hour. A radio reporter, squashed against Evonne, who sat huddled in a folding chair next to Margaret, shoved his microphone across her chest until it was resting on Court's chin. What did she think about the boos some of the fans had let out when a tournament official had mentioned, at the closing ceremony, that for the first time the women's prize money was equal to the men's?

"I've never been a women's libber," Margaret said softly, "but I'm very happy to win that amount. I feel maybe women don't have the depth the men do, and men have to play five sets, but the women are drawing as many people as the men here. . . ."

It was a signal for the inevitable questions. What about Billie Jean? What about Bobby Riggs?

"I'd like her to win," came the sweet, singsong reply. "Of course, if Billie Jean loses, I'll challenge him again. . . ." On and on it went. The crown was hers, but Margaret was queen only for a day. The twin shadows of a little old bespectacled man and a little young bespectacled woman that had hung over her all week refused to fade.

An hour later, she emerged from the locker room, a bottle of beer in one hand, little Danny clutching the other. A few onlookers on the veranda casually paid their respects. Barry picked up her big black carryall. They left. On the way out, a girl passed by them, wearing a T-shirt that said "Love Billie, zero Bobby."

Margaret Court had just won her fifth Forest Hills singles title, her 97-zillionth international championship . . . and nobody seemed to care.

You've Come a Long Way, Billie

IT WAS THE DAY BEFORE THE BATTLE OF THE SEXES, AND the Astrodome complex had turned into one vast gambling casino.

Each night in the practice bubble, Bobby Riggs had taken on a different challenger for an average of $100 a set, first spotting them a few games or setting out rows of folding chairs on the court to liven things up. He had won every time. In keeping with the all-American free enterprise commercialism of the event, spectators were charged $5 admission just to watch the practice sessions. Bobby's victims had included Denton Cooley, the heart surgeon (Bobby had also won from him a free checkup for his brother John, a cardiac patient) and Larry King, who was coaxed onto the court by Jerry Perenchio, the match promoter, as a gimmick to hype ticket sales.

But Bobby was not the only one making book. Perenchio staked $1,000 on Billie Jean with Sid Shlenker, the Astrodome boss. Rosie Casals, who was to do the color commentary on television with Howard Cosell, laid out a few thousand with a Vegas bookie. Bill Moffitt, Billie Jean's ruggedly handsome father, had a few thousand on the line back in California with some fellow firemen. Jimmy the Greek spent hours on the telephone.

The press corps went simply out of control. Writers around the dinner table were like alcoholics let loose in the

Jack Daniels distillery—before the appetizers arrived there would be piles of $5 bills stacked between the butter dish and the bread bowl, while some of the most sophisticated reporters in the country sat frantically composing arcane number combinations on scraps of paper. There were pools on how many games the winner would lose, how many games the loser would win—just about the only pool overlooked was one on how many tubas the band would have playing the National Anthem.

When the final, big writers' pool was tallied on Wednesday, the verdict was 22 for Riggs, 10 for King.

There was no way, the experts agreed, that Bobby could lose.

Only one person in town, it seemed, had no betting money on the match: Billie Jean King. "Gambling doesn't turn me on," she said calmly, sitting in the practice bubble Wednesday in a lime-green warm-up suit.

Was there something else at stake at this Reno-style carnival besides money? someone asked.

She took a deep breath. "Pride."

On all the slips of paper I had contributed to the pools, I had written "BJK" but it had been with a shaky hand. I wanted her to win more than I had wanted anybody to win anything since Johnny Podres had thrown the last pitch in the '55 Series, not just because I had written a front page paean for *The New York Times* Sunday sports section predicting a four-set King victory, not just because I had gambled half my plane fare home, but because in spite of her faults Billie Jean represented the best that women's sports had to offer. A few weeks before, Nora Ephron (who was putting her money on Bobby now, even though she was the treasurer of our side bet against him) had remarked, "Billie Jean's not the feminist she says she is." Nora was right, of course, but who among us was? Billie Jean had come a long way, as an athlete and as a feminist, and I didn't want her to let us down now.

She was not making it easy to pull for her, however.

Since playing her two tournament matches at the Net-Set Racquet Club on Monday and working out the next two nights in the bubble briefly, Billie Jean had virtually gone into seclusion. And while Bobby had gamboled, Billie Jean had trained.

Each night, after dinner, she had forced herself to stay awake later and later, so that she would rise later the next morning. The match was scheduled for 7 P.M. and she wanted to be out of bed for seven hours—no more—when that time came. Each day, she did sit-ups, lifted her knee weights, ate a big breakfast of an omelette or ham and eggs, watched television, joked with her father. (One evening they kiddingly compared biceps. Moffitt, who kept reminding everyone he was the same age as Riggs, recalled that he had played three sets of tennis for fun recently against his daughter. He laughed. "She tired me out so much I had to stay in bed two days!")

The night before the match, Billie Jean and Dennis van der Meer, King's longtime coach who had also been Margaret Court's coach at the Mother's Day Massacre, sat in King's Houston Oaks hotel suite like Joe Namath and Weeb Ewbank, screening the film of the Riggs-Court match while Marilyn Barnett carefully took notes on their dialogue.

Billie Jean paid particular attention to Riggs's backhand. With typical King *chutzpah,* she had solicited advice on Bobby's game from the woman she had called a "donkey," and Margaret had told her his backhand was his weak spot.

The next morning, her mood swung like a pendulum from, as she put it, " 'I'm ready' to 'El Foldo.' " She and Marilyn went to a supermarket to buy some Gatorade. An elderly lady spotted her. "I hope," she said, "that you beat his pompous ass!" Billie Jean roared. She returned to the hotel and danced around the suite to the music of "Jesus Christ Superstar." Larry King told her he figured the match would go four sets. "No," she corrected him. "Three."

At the Astrodome, a group of celebrities flown in from

Hollywood by Perenchio including Jim Brown, Andy Williams and Sandra Giles (Bobby's starlet girlfriend) whiled away the afternoon playing exhibition matches for a sparse crowd. (The evening's tickets entitled them to the afternoon's entertainment as well.) When Billie Jean showed up, she headed straight for the visiting team locker room, which she had requested because her brother, Randy Moffitt, the San Francisco Giants pitcher, used it. The rather bare, cinder-block main room contained a banquet table laid out with food for the women celebrities. Billie Jean dressed in the manager's room, but before she left the Dome that night she tacked a note on locker 20. The Giants would be in town the following week to play the Astros. The note read: "Hi, Randy—BJK."

The Old Lady was ready.

Cecil B. De Mille, Walt Disney, Pete Rozelle and the Emperor Nero working as a team could not have staged it better.

A glittering crowd of 30,472 people in everything from evening gowns to dungarees milled around the corridors of the Astrodome, browsing through souvenir stands selling $5 commemorative racquet covers with drawings of Bobby and Billie on either side, tennis sweatbands with the biological symbol for women on them, patches of Astroturf.

Like a green, elongated prizefight ring, the court sat squarely in the infield surrounded by yellow folding chairs, with a champagne bar and a carving board cart offering slices of hot roast beef strategically located in the corners. Midgets dressed as dancing bears frolicked near the dugouts, the University of Houston marching band thumped out "Jesus Christ Superstar," a dozen cheerleaders in red hot pants swirled pompons, two dozen women tennis pros in BJK T-shirts lined up along a red carpet outside the field entrance screeching fight songs, and a fortyish woman with a diamond-encrusted cross hanging between breasts bulging out of a white floor-length peignoir slithered into a front row seat.

From the rafters of the middle tiers of red and orange seats hung an array of banners—"East West North South Ms. King Gonna Close Bobby's Mouth," "Oconomowoc, Wisc. Says Beat Him Billie Jean."

Then, to a trumpet flourish, with Howard Cosell giving a play-by-play in a glass-enclosed booth at one corner of the court, a feathered litter right out of *Cleopatra* carried by bare-chested muscle men emerged from beneath the stands onto the carpet. Numero Uno herself, a fixed smile on her face, a lime-green sweater covering her rhinestone-studded blue-and-green Tinling dress, waved at her subjects like an elementary school kid who has suddenly found herself in the middle of the Rose Bowl parade. (Much later, she held a framed photograph of that moment in her hands and muttered, "At that point, it was El Barfo.")

Another trumpet flourish, and a Chinese rickshaw on gold wheels pulled by a gaggle of girls known as Bobby's Bosom Buddies, their chests heaving against their sweaters like miniature dirigibles, emerged along the second carpet. In it sat the Happy Hustler, cradling a mammoth Sugar Daddy to his own bosom, his small frame practically hidden from view by what seemed like 900 shoving photographers.

Sitting in a tuxedo in the front row next to heavyweight champion George Foreman, Jerry Perenchio ran a steady hand over his Beverly Hills razor cut and said contentedly, "It's the fight crowd. It's ancient Rome. It's the closest I've come to getting a woman and a man in the ring together."

A few rows back, Bill Moffitt turned to a reporter. "I want him shut up," he said, gesturing at Riggs. "If he tries anything funny I'm gonna punch him." Suddenly, out of the corner of his eye, he saw Billie Jean smack a practice volley past Bobby. "Go, baby, GO!" he shouted, leaping out of his seat.

From the second she won the toss, Billie Jean was in command. All the Barfos, Chokos, Foldos, blood tests and bitcheries were behind her. King was where she belonged, poised on the toes of her blue suede BJK Adidas sneakers with her upturned little nose nearly hanging over the net, her muscular right arm holding her BJK Wilson racquet cocked for a crunching backhand volley, with 30,000 screaming fans going bananas under the spider-web girders of Houston's gift to architectural vulgarity.

It was tennis the way she had always wanted it, on prime time television, before a viewing audience of 37 million people, many of them, incredibly, seeing a professional match for the very first time.

In the first game, the two players were feeling each other out. Billie Jean, glancing up nervously at the lights bouncing off the roof, served tentatively, concentrating simply on keeping her balls in play. She wanted Bobby to make the errors, to impress upon him from the outset that she would not crack like Margaret when his chip shots spun off the carpet. She wanted to establish her confidence immediately. At ad-in she hit a crunching high backhand volley, one of her most devastating shots, to win the game. The crowd, which had roared at every practice winner King had hit during the warm-up, bellowed its approval as the two came to the sideline for the changeover.

Bobby Riggs slumped in his chair at the sidelines while his Boy Friday, Lornie Kuhle, massaged his legs. He turned around and spotted Dick Butera, the Hilton Head Racquet Club president, who had tried to talk him into a $10,000 bet at 2 to 1 just before the match. Bobby had refused, demanding 8 to 5. Now, down one game, he sent Lornie to Butera's seat. "Bobby says he'll take 2 to 1," Lornie told him.

It was to be his final, quixotic fling. Billie Jean retook the court for the second game with an extra spring in her step. As the set progressed, her strokes grew bolder, more authoritative, as if she were repeating to herself, "This is where I belong." Bobby, looking tense and comical at the same time in his Sugar Daddy warm-up jacket, was not where he belonged. He was running like a geriatric jackrabbit from one side of the court to the other, sweeping futilely at a dazzling selection of King spins, chops, smashes. At 4-5, the nerveless wonder, the man with all the angles, the guy who knew how to keep a hold on himself with the eyes of the world on him, choked. Bobby Riggs double-faulted to give Billie Jean the set, and in the first row, George Foreman was on his feet, both black fists in the air.

"Atta boy, Billie!" thundered the champ.

No fans were getting hoarser more quickly than Billie Jean's sister pros, jammed together in a corner of "ringside," some in chairs, some squatting on the sideline carpet.

"Kill 'em, kill 'em!" yelled Kerry Melville, the quietest little churchmouse on the Slims circuit. "Cheat a little!" yelled sixteen-year-old Kathy Kuykendall at Deedee Dalley, the lineswoman nearest the corner. "My eyeballs are floating," said Nancy Richey Gunter, once King's arch rival, as she tipsily stumbled to her feet to search for a bathroom. When she returned, weaving, she noticed that there was a discernible stain of red on the seat of Bobby's shorts. "Maybe he's getting his period!" she howled.

Directly behind the baseline, Gladys Heldman sat with a glass of champagne in her hand next to Teddy Tinling. "We're all going crazy," Gladys said with a big smile, her voice an even deeper baritone than usual. "The hustler out-hustled himself. I'm sitting next to a lovely male chauvinist. What a wonderful time we're having!"

Stella Lachowicz of Virginia Slims passed by, wordlessly handing out small pink pieces of paper with printing on them. They were invitations to a Bobby Riggs Pasadena Bridge Jump.

Easing up just a little at the start of the second set, Billie Jean had trouble with her first serve and let Bobby break her in the first game. It didn't matter. She broke him right back in the next game, and in the glass-enclosed broadcasting booth, Rosie Casals smiled at Riggs's distress. "Like a duck out of water," she remarked.

Billie Jean was forcing him now, forcing him to come to the net and play her game, passing him with bullet-like ground strokes down the line, wrong-footing him at the baseline. Huddled in the corner beneath Cosell's booth, Bud Collins and Neil Amdur wrote furiously in tiny notebooks, their eyes wide with disbelief. "Nothing but winners," murmured Neil. "She's hitting nothing but winners."

They stayed even through the seventh game, but the serve-and-volley pace was taking its toll heavily on the old man. His famed lobs had become inviting targets for Billie Jean's unflinching overheads, his first serve refused to stay within the service line and his second serve was skittering straight to King's fearsome backhand. After failing to take advantage of two break points in the fourth game and a third in the sixth game, she carved up Bobby's service in the eighth, first with a sliced backhand, then a topspin forehand, then a backhand return-of-serve passing shot. It was 5-3, Billie Jean.

Marilyn Barnett, in a brown-and-blue paisley halter-dress ("In yoga," she had explained to me, "brown is for money and blue is for spirit"), was sitting totally calm next to the Gatorade cooler in Billie Jean's row of sideline chairs. As Billie Jean served for the second set, Marilyn looked across the court at the Slims corner, smiled beatifically, and, with her thumb and forefinger, formed a small circle.

The third set began with Billie Jean breaking Bobby in the very first game, then holding her own in the second game for an insurmountable 2-0 lead. She had won five straight games. Could Billie Jean keep up the pace? She let down enough for him to win the third game and then break back in the fourth. But with the score at 2-2, a rubber-kneed Riggs began running around his backhand and Billie Jean broke his serve again, this time at love. When the score reached 4-2 King, Bobby suddenly stopped the action, coming to the sidelines to have his aching fingers massaged. What no one knew at the time was that Billie Jean herself had suddenly developed leg cramps. "Oh God —not now!" she thought silently. Bobby returned to the court and won the next game on two unforced errors by

King to make it 4-3. Billie steeled herself against the cramps: 15-0, 15-15, 30-15, 40-15, game. The score was 5-3. One more and the circus would be over.

With Bobby serving, the game went to 30-all. Billie Jean dropped a ball right at Bobby's feet on the next serve, and the crowd leaped up in anticipation. Match point. But Bobby wasn't ready to give up, winning the next two points to take the advantage. The game went to deuce twice again before Billie Jean got another chance at match point on a flashing backhand down the line. Still she couldn't finish him off, and twice more they went to deuce.

It ended as it had begun, in Felliniesque pandemonium. Bobby double-faulted to give King her third nerve-wracking, spine-tingling match point. A weak Riggs serve . . . a short exchange . . . and Bobby's high backhand volley sailed harmlessly into the net. The electronic tote-board flashed the numbers 6-4, 6-3, 6-3. A wooden object sailed high toward the roof—Billie Jean's racquet. Before the stampede of fans and reporters could reach her, she shook Bobby's hand, kissed Dennis van der Meer, kissed Dick Butera and fell into Larry's arms. His cherubic cheeks pale, his hands shaking, Larry lifted her onto a table at courtside while Perenchio handed her a trophy and Foreman gave her a check.

Billie Jean blew kisses at the cameras, stuck her tongue out at Van der Meer, held up a fist to Marilyn. As the trophy was put in her hands, she spied her father standing in the crush.

Billie Jean shoved the trophy in his direction, holding it over her head. "Thanks, Daddy!" she shouted above the din.

"Way to go, champ!" he shouted back.

The insane eleven-year-old I had seen at Wimbledon was back.

She unlaced her sneakers, plopped them on top of the table set up on a platform in the home dressing room for the post-match interview, asked for a beer, and marched back and forth like a wind-up tin soldier. "Gotta calm myself down first," she told the assembled press corps, a group now large enough to staff four mass circulation dailies and the three TV networks besides.

I realized that I was having trouble breathing as I put my tape recorder up on the table. Billie Jean looked down at me. "Didya win a lot of money, Grace?" she demanded.

"Yes, thank you, Billie Jean," I stammered. Then, remembering a comment of hers, I added, "But it's not the money, it's the pride."

"Right on!" She grinned.

The interview began in earnest with someone asking her feelings about the conquest. "I feel this is the culmination of nineteen years in tennis. . . ." she began. I sneaked out of the room to file my story. It was a speech I knew almost by heart, and it was beside the point. The point was that when the chips were down, a twenty-nine-year-old woman athlete, Billie Jean King Superstar, had hung tough. I was so happy I wanted to cry.

While everybody else in Houston stayed up most of the night getting loaded, Billie Jean paid a brief visit to Jerry Perenchio's party in the Astroworld penthouse and then went back to the Oaks with her parents to watch an old Claudette Colbert movie on television.

The next day, she was back at the Net-Set, to play another round in the Virginia Slims tournament. A big bouquet of roses was waiting for her from the players, who only a week before had been angrily talking about having the Women's Tennis Association fine her for skipping too many recent tournaments. They were glad Astrotennis was over; so was she. "Anyone who had to live with the day-to-day pressure of playing that match wouldn't want to go through it again," she admitted. "You can't go out, you can't eat in a restaurant, you stop living." She smiled. "Now I want to live a little."

A knot of people had gathered around her, still wanting to know what Astrotennis really meant.

"Maybe it means that people will start to respect women athletes more," she said. "But it's not just me. There are plenty more to take my place. And in the next decade, I think you'll see women athletes finally getting the attention they've deserved all along."

It was a fine summation, presented in the tones of a stateswoman. A little while later, I asked her what she thought about one incredible statistic from the Riggs match. She had hit 64 percent outright winners, balls placed so well Bobby never got his racquet on them.

"Wow!" She grinned. "That's like pitchin' a no-hit game!"

And she did a slow, perfect pantomime of a pitcher, rearing back for the high hard one.